PROPHETS OF GOD AND FALSE PROPHETS

TRUE AND FALSE TEACHINGS

LESLIE M. JOHN

PROPHETS OF GOD AND FALSE PROPHETS

TRUE AND FALSE TEACHINGS

LESLIE M. JOHN

My mission is to proclaim the good news of our Lord Jesus Christ as revealed to me through Holy Bible and from various teachers, preachers, and commentators. This is my voluntary service to God in the name of His only begotten Son Lord Jesus Christ.

I share the truth of knowledge of God with others with good intention of bringing them to the knowledge of the living God, the God of Abraham, the God of Isaac, the God of Jacob, and the Father of our Lord Jesus Christ. My mission is to proclaim the Gospel of Lord Jesus Christ and not converting forcibly anyone to Christianity. One may accept or reject any or part of my writings/teachings.

This book presents true teachings of Lord Jesus Christ and false teachings, as I understand.. No offence is meant towards any person, religion, or organization. All Scriptures are taken from KJV from open domain.

ISBN-10:0989028380
ISBN-13:978-0-9890283-8-7

Table of Contents

PREFACE

The whole Bible is centered on Lord Jesus Christ who is the Savior of mankind. In all the sixty six books of Bible Lord Jesus Christ is seen as the redeemer. Whoever believes Him as the Savior and confesses sins to Him will have everlasting life.

"Jesus answered and said unto him, Verily, verily, I say unto thee, Except a man be born again, he cannot see the kingdom of God". John 3:3

They parted his garments, they scourged him, they hurled insults on him and crucified along with two thieves; yet Jesus was so kind on those who crucified them.

"Then said Jesus, Father, forgive them; for they know not what they do. And they parted his raiment, and cast lots". Luke 23:34

Jesus also forgave one of the thieves who were crucified along with him, when the thief made prayer to him to remember him when Jesus comes into His Kingdom.

"And Jesus said unto him, Verily I say unto thee, To day shalt thou be with me in paradise". Luke 23:43

On the third day Lord Jesus Christ rose from the dead and after forty days He ascended into heaven. He is seated at the right of the Majesty.

"For if we believe that Jesus died and rose again, even so them also which sleep in Jesus will God bring with him". 1 Thessalonians 4:14

Jesus died upon the cross of Calvary so that we may be reconciled unto Him. There is no difference, whether we are Jews or Gentiles; He died for all of us, and rose from the dead and ascended in to heaven. We, who were His enemies, are made His children. The opposition that was caused between Heaven and Earth by our committing sins is removed once and for all, by the appeasement of our sins by Jesus Christ dying on the cross for our sake. We are reconciled unto God through His blood that was shed upon the cross of Calvary.

If you have not accepted Jesus Christ as your personal Savior, today is the day of Salvation. Please accept Jesus Christ as your personal Savior, and your Lord, to enter in to the Kingdom of God.

Jesus saith unto him, I am the way, the truth, and the life: no man cometh unto the Father, but by me". John 14:6

"For all have sinned, and come short of the glory of God;" Romans 3:23

Salvation is available freely for all who believe in Jesus Christ, and confess his/her sins to Him, and accept Jesus Christ as his/her personal Savior and also acknowledge Him as his/her Lord. Today is the day of salvation. Please confess your sins to Jesus Christ and be blessed. Receive Salvation and eternal life.

Jesus is the Way, the truth, and the life. If you confess your sins to Jesus, and express faith in your heart that he died for you sins and rose from the dead, accept Him as your personal savior, and acknowledge with your mouth that he is your Lord, you will also be received in to Paradise immediately after your days on this earth.

INTRODUCTION

There are many Bible teachers in the world and it is hard to differentiate the true teachings of Lord Jesus Christ and false teachings from the Adversary, the Satan. Bible says in the last days there will be many false prophets and false teachers leading astray the innocents from the truth.

Bible asks us to test who is of the Lord and who is not.

WHO IS OF GOD AND WHO IS NOT?

"Wherefore I give you to understand, that no man speaking by the Spirit of God calleth Jesus accursed: and that no man can say that Jesus is the Lord, but by the Holy Ghost" 1 Corinthians 12:3)

Apostle Paul affirms with much confidence that no one can say that Jesus is the Lord except by the conviction of Holy Spirit and such a one who has in him Holy Spirit indwelling would not call Jesus as accursed. There are many who profess the name of the Lord Jesus Christ and yet they do not confess His deity. They might project Jesus as a good man, prophet, and a good teacher but when it comes to confessing that Lord Jesus Christ is the Son of God incarnated and came down into this world and lived among us they withdraw with excuses; they pretend to be Christians inducing wrong teaching and never acknowledging that the Word became flesh and lived among us.

John 1:14 says that "...the Word was made flesh and dwelt among us..." It is very important to observe whether or not a person acknowledges that the Word was made flesh and lived among us. If a person speaks otherwise and/or does not acknowledge Lord Jesus Christ's deity and His human nature when He was in this world surely the said person is not of God.

It was not only once emphasized in the Scripture but this fact was emphasized several times. God honored and will continue to honor all those who acknowledge Lord Jesus Christ as the Messiah. Peter acknowledged that Jesus was the Messiah (John 1:41) and, therefore, Jesus honored him saying "that he shall be called Cephas..."

"And he brought him to Jesus. And when Jesus beheld him, he said, Thou art Simon the son of Jona: thou shalt be called Cephas, which is by interpretation, A stone". (John 1:42)

John 21:16-17 shows how Jesus had a close conversation with Peter and when he was questioned whether or not he loved Him Peter said "yea" and rightly as he deserved Jesus said to him "Feed my sheep".

We are saved by grace through faith in Lord Jesus Christ and salvation is gift of God. Salvation is by Lord Jesus Christ and none else and it is not of any good works done by us.

Our good works and righteousness are like filthy rags before God. Our fight in this world is not against any man but with Satan. Paul writes in Ephesians 6:12 that we wrestle in the world not with flesh and blood but against principalities, against powers, and against the rulers of the darkness of this world and against spiritual wickedness in high places

John's first epistle chapter 4 and 5 contain vital information and it forms the basis to have it as a definition while identifying as to who is of God and who is not of God.

"Hereby know ye the Spirit of God: Every spirit that confesseth that Jesus Christ is come in the flesh is of God. And every spirit that confesseth not that Jesus Christ is come in the flesh is not of God: and this is that [spirit] of antichrist, whereof ye have heard that it should come; and even now already is it in the world." (1 John 4:2, 3)

"Whosoever shall confess that Jesus is the Son of God, God dwelleth in him, and he in God". (1 John 4:15)

"And we know that the Son of God is come, and hath given us an understanding, that we may know him that is true, and we are in him that is true, even in his Son Jesus Christ. This is the true God, and eternal life". (1 John 5:20)

In the New Testament there are many verses where the word 'false' occurs. It is noticeable that the word 'false' is always associated with some other word such as "False prophets", "False witness", "False Christ", "False accusation", "False apostles", "False teachers"

Whenever there is a dispute about interpretation of scriptures it is imperative that we refer to the words in 'Hebrew' in the case of Old Testament and 'Greek' in the case of New Testament.

But there were false prophets also among the people, even as there shall be false teachers among you, who privily shall bring in damnable heresies, even denying the Lord that bought them, and bring upon themselves swift destruction. And many shall follow their pernicious ways; by reason of whom the way of truth shall be evil spoken of. (2 Peter 2:1-2)

Words namely 'damnable', 'destruction' and 'pernicious' used in 2 Peter 2:1-2 are the transliterated word of Greek Strong's number 684 is 'apoleia' which means 'perdition'. This word is used in

"The beast that thou sawest was, and is not; and shall ascend out of the bottomless pit, and go into perdition: and they that dwell on the earth shall wonder, whose names were not written in the book of life from the foundation of the world, when they behold the beast that was, and is not, and yet is". (Revelation 17:8)

"And the beast that was, and is not, even he is the eighth, and is of the seven, and goeth into perdition" (Revelation 17:11)

Those who are false prophets and/or false teachers come under this category. They teach damnable heresies and denying the deity of Lord Jesus Christ. They never acknowledge that the 'word' became flesh and lived among us.

The same came to Jesus by night, and said unto him, Rabbi, we know that thou art a teacher come from God: for no man can do these miracles that thou doest, except God be with him. (John 3:2)

An instructor of the foolish, a teacher of babes, which hast the form of knowledge and of the truth in the law. (Romans 2:20)

Whereunto I am ordained a preacher, and an apostle, (I speak the truth in Christ, and lie not;) a teacher of the Gentiles in faith and verity. (1 Timothy 2:7)

Whereunto I am appointed a preacher, and an apostle, and a teacher of the Gentiles. (2 Timothy 1:11)

One verse for example:

And when they had gone through the isle unto Paphos, they found a certain sorcerer, a false prophet, a Jew, whose name was Barjesus: (Acts 13:6)

Barjesus was a false prophet, a sorcerer. He was a fortune teller of future events.

The Scripture clearly says it is not for us to know the time of Lord Jesus Christ's return, and yet man's curiosity runs helter skelter to calculate the day of His return. Not a surprise, every time Lord Jesus Christ's second coming was prophesied by men they were proved beyond doubt fake prophets

In the Old Testament periods such false prophets were to be put to death.

"If there arise among you a prophet, or a dreamer of dreams, and giveth thee a sign or a wonder, And the sign or the wonder come to pass, whereof he spake unto thee, saying, Let us go after other gods, which thou hast not known, and let us serve them; Thou shalt not hearken unto the words of that prophet, or that dreamer of dreams: for the LORD your God proveth you, to know whether ye love the LORD your God with all your heart and with all your soul. Ye shall walk after the LORD your God, and fear him, and keep his commandments, and obey his voice, and ye shall serve him, and cleave unto him. And that prophet, or that dreamer of dreams, shall be put to death; because he hath spoken to turn you away from the LORD your God, which brought you out of the land of Egypt, and redeemed you out of the house of bondage, to thrust thee out of the way which the LORD thy God commanded thee to walk in. So shalt thou put the evil away from the midst of thee". (Deuteronomy 13:1-5)

Moses was a type of Lord Jesus Christ and he was a mediator between the children of Israel and God. Likewise Lord Jesus Christ is our mediator between us and the Father. The scripture say that if prophecy from a prophet is not a true prophet and he shall be put to death (Ref: *Deuteronomy 18:15-22)*

Jesus warned about such false prophets:

"Beware of false prophets, which come to you in sheep's clothing, but inwardly they are ravening wolves". (Matthew 7:15)

Apostle Paul warned of false prophets:

"Take heed therefore unto yourselves, and to all the flock, over the which the Holy Ghost hath made you overseers, to feed the church of God, which he hath purchased with his own blood. For I know this, that after my departing shall grievous wolves enter in among you, not sparing the flock. Also of your own selves shall men arise, speaking perverse things, to draw away disciples after them". (Acts 20:28-30)

Apostle Paul pointed to the false prophets and false preachers:

"For such are false apostles, deceitful workers, transforming themselves into the apostles of Christ. And no marvel; for Satan himself is transformed into an angel of light" (2 Corinthians 11:13-14)

Jude warned about such false prophets and false teachers

"For there are certain men crept in unawares, who were before of old ordained to this condemnation, ungodly men, turning the

grace of our God into lasciviousness, and denying the only Lord God, and our Lord Jesus Christ". (Jude 1:4)

There are many more verses that show that whenever Bible speaks about false prophets and false teachers it always referred to those who deny the deity of Lord Jesus Christ.

In 2 Peter 2 false prophets and false teachers refer to those who bring in damnable heresies denying the deity of Lord Jesus Christ, not of other interpretational differences of opinions.

CHAPTER 1
HOW DID GOD SPEAK TO MAN?

"God, who at sundry times and in divers manners spake in time past unto the fathers by the prophets, Hath in these last days spoken unto us by his Son, whom he hath appointed heir of all things, by whom also he made the worlds; Who being the brightness of his glory, and the express image of his person, and upholding all things by the word of his power, when he had by himself purged our sins, sat down on the right hand of the Majesty on high" (Hebrews 1:1-3)

God spoke to Adam, Abraham, Moses and many other prophets in the Old Testament period and to many in the New Testament period and to many after His resurrection and ascension.

From Genesis account it is clear that God had a perfect relationship with Adam and He walked in the cool of the day in the Garden of Eden. Adam transgressed the commandment of God and hid himself when God inquired of him as to where he was. Adam said he was naked, and, therefore, he hid from God.

Adam knew that he was naked only after he transgressed the commandment of God. God covered Adam with the skin of a dead animal by removing the apron he made for himself with the leaves by his own works. His works to cover his nakedness was not enough in the sight of God and He made His own provision for covering the nakedness of Adam.

During this period much conversation took place between God and Adam. God expelled Adam and Eve from the Garden of Eden in order that he may not lay hands on the tree of life.

Man fell from the presence of God and man's posterity could not see the glory of God from then onwards until Lord Jesus Christ, who was with Father, came into this world in the form of servant in the likeness of man to redeem him from the bondage of sin provided he repented of his sin and to reconcile man with the Father.

God spoke to Moses from the burning bush.

"And when the LORD saw that he turned aside to see, God called unto him out of the midst of the bush, and said, Moses, Moses. And he said, Here am I" Exodus 3:4

God spoke to Moses, His servant and Aaron, the high priest from "Mercy Seat" in the Tabernacle. God spoke to Abraham by coming in the form of man. God spoke to prophets through visions and in dreams. Lord Jesus was present with Shadrach, Meshach, and Abednego in fiery furnace(Christophany).

GOD SPOKE THROUGH HIS SON

"Hath in these last days spoken unto us by [his] Son, whom he hath appointed heir of all things, by whom also he made the worlds" Hebrews 1:2

Lord Jesus Christ spoke about the Father and said He and the Father are one and whoever has seen Him has seen the Father. The Son of God, Lord Jesus Christ, relinquished His glory in heaven, and came into this world. The Father, The Son, and The Holy Spirit are one and co-equal and co-existence. Lord Jesus Christ is the way, the truth and the life.

"I and my Father are one." John 10:30

"No man can come to me, except the Father which hath sent me draw him: and I will raise him up at the last day" John 6:44

"For he hath made him [to be] sin for us, who knew no sin; that we might be made the righteousness of God in him" 2 Corinthians 5:21

Lord Jesus Christ, the Son of God, became mediator between the Father and man to give man salvation. Lord Jesus Christ paid the price of redemption of man by taking upon Him the sin of man and dying on the cross. His blood cleanses us from our sin provided we repent of our sins.

In the New Testament period before Jesus ascended into heaven he spoke in person face to face to some.

"Jesus saith unto her, Woman, why weepest thou? whom seekest thou? She, supposing him to be the gardener, saith unto him, Sir, if thou have borne him hence, tell me where thou hast laid him, and I will take him away" John 20:15

After Lord Jesus Christ is seated at the right hand of the Majesty Holy Spirit came into this world to be with His disciples and with all those who believed Him as Savior. The Holy Spirit dwelt in the believers as soon as they accepted Jesus as their Savior. In the present age God speaks to us from His Holy Word and the Spirit who speaks strongly to us in our hearts convicting us the truth and providing way to escape from sinning. God also speaks through preachers, teachers of the Word of God and sometimes also from the mouths of our closed ones, if they were believers in Lord Jesus Christ and had salvation.

In the kingdom age when Lord Jesus Christ comes He will speak to those who were justified as righteous during "Great

Tribulation Period" and justified as righteous in the "Sheep and Goat judgment" in the same way as He spoke to His disciples and others after His resurrection from the dead. Every eye will see Lord Jesus Christ and acknowledge that He is Lord Jesus Christ, the Son of God, and the Savior.

"Behold, he cometh with clouds; and every eye shall see him, and they also which pierced him: and all kindreds of the earth shall wail because of him. Even so, Amen"(Revelation 1:7)

GOD SPOKE IN SMALL STILL VOICE

"And after the earthquake a fire; [but] the LORD [was] not in the fire: and after the fire a still small voice" 1 Kings 19:12

During the journey of Israelites in the wilderness God spoke to Moses several times. One such incidence is found in Exodus 19:16-19. There were thunders and lightening and a thick cloud upon the Mount Sinai The trumpet sound was exceedingly loud and the people trembled. While the people waited near the Mount Sinai God descended upon it in fire and some ascended as the smoke from a furnace. Mount Sinai was on a smoke and God responded to Moses in a voice.

In 1 Kings 18:20-40 there is a dramatic presentation of how Elijah proved that Jehovah is the real God, the God of heaven and earth, the God who created heavens, earth, seas and all that is therein. Baal and four hundred and fifty prophets of Baal were humiliated and Elijah killed them all. The idol remained an idol speechless. God showed up on Mount Carmel in the form of fire and consumed the burnt sacrifice offered by Elijah.

Elijah was afraid of the threatening made by Jezebel, wife of wicked king, Ahab. She threatened to kill Elijah, and somehow Elijah's fear exceeded the success he had seen earlier. He went and hid in a cave where an angel of the Lord appeared to him and asked him to be courageous, rise and eat. Elijah obeyed and rose and ate for forty days and forty nights on the mount.

The LORD said to Elijah to stand upon the mount and Elijah did as the LORD said to him. God passed by and behold there was great and strong wind rent the mountains and broke the rocks but He was not there. After this an earthquake took place and after earthquake a fire, but the LORD was not in the fire, but after the fire there God came to Elijah in a small still voice and spoke to him.

The word of the LORD came to Elijah and asked him "What doest thou here, Elijah?" Prophet Elijah answered the LORD God of hosts that he was very jealous for the LORD and while the children of Israel forsook the covenant, he was all alone left to stand for the LORD and his life is being sought after. God said to Elijah that there were He reserved seven thousand in Israel who did not bow their knees to Baal.

"Yet I have left [me] seven thousand in Israel, all the knees which have not bowed unto Baal, and every mouth which hath not kissed him" 1 Kings 19:18

In the following references we see that God spoke in fire, thunder, whirlwind besides speaking in still small voice.

Job 37:2 "Hear attentively the noise of his voice, and the sound [that] goeth out of his mouth"

Job 38:1 "Then the LORD answered Job out of the whirlwind, and said" Psalm 104:7 "At thy rebuke they fled; at the voice of thy thunder they hasted away.

Zechariah 4:6 Then he answered and spake unto me, saying, This [is] the word of the LORD unto Zerubbabel, saying, Not by might, nor by power, but by my spirit, saith the LORD of hosts"

John 12:29 "The people therefore, that stood by, and heard [it], said that it thundered: others said, An angel spake to him"

"And out of the throne proceeded lightnings and thunderings and voices: and [there were] seven lamps of fire burning before the throne, which are the seven Spirits of God" Revelation 4:5

Thus we see that God spoke to man in different ways in different periods and the writer of Hebrews rightly said:

GOD SPOKE THROUGH PROPHETS

"God, who at sundry times and in divers manners spake in time past unto the fathers by the prophets, Hath in these last days spoken unto us by [his] Son, whom he hath appointed heir of all things, by whom also he made the worlds" Hebrews 1:1-2

CHAPTER 2
THE GOD OF ISRAEL

God chose Israel as His nation and the offspring of Jacob as His people. It is about these people, the Israelites that the Bible speaks most about. The prophets spoke about the chastisement of Israel because of her worship of Baal and Ashtaroth, their Babylonian captivity for seventy years as a consequence of their failure to keep Sabbath, and their future.

God in His mercy accommodated the Gentiles to be partakers of the blessings of Israel and gave them the equal heritage through Lord Jesus Christ, the Son of God, the incarnate God, who relinquished His glory with the Father and came into this world, dwelt among men, did miracles, died on behalf of men, taking upon Him the sin of man, that whoever believes in Him shall not perish but have everlasting life.

Even though Prophets spoke in diverse manner in diverse periods of time they did not know the mystery of the Church, the body of Christ, whose members are the believers in Him and He is the head. The Church was a mystery and it is revealed only in the New Testament.

"How that by revelation he made known unto me the mystery; (as I wrote afore in few words, Whereby, when ye read, ye may understand my knowledge in the mystery of Christ) Which in other ages was not made known unto the sons of men, as it is now revealed unto his holy apostles and prophets by the Spirit; That the Gentiles should be fellowheirs, and of the same body,

and partakers of his promise in Christ by the gospel" Ephesians 3:3-6

"God, who at sundry times and in divers manners spake in time past unto the fathers by the prophets, Hath in these last days spoken unto us by [his] Son, whom he hath appointed heir of all things, by whom also he made the worlds; Who being the brightness of [his] glory, and the express image of his person, and upholding all things by the word of his power, when he had by himself purged our sins, sat down on the right hand of the Majesty on high; Being made so much better than the angels, as he hath by inheritance obtained a more excellent name than they" Hebrews 1:1-4

There were nine prophets who spoke before the captivity of Israel, four during the period of captivity of Israel and three after their release from captivity. However, God is yet to deal with Israel fully.

The Nine prophets who spoke before the captivity of Israel were:

1. Jonah
2. Joel
3. Hosea
4. Amos
5. Micah
6. Isaiah
7. Nahum
8. Zephaniah
9. Habakkuk

The four prophets who spoke during the captivity of Israel were:

1. Jeremiah
2. Daniel
3. Ezekiel
4. Obadiah

The three prophets who spoke after the return of Israel from their captivity were:

1. Micah
2. Zechariah
3. Malachi

In the last days God spoke through His only begotten Son, Lord Jesus Christ, as written in Hebrews 1:1-4. The return of Israelites is not complete and the "fullness of time" by which the accommodating the Gentiles in the Church is known only to God.

Bible speaks about this mystery as we read in Romans 11th Chapter, especially a very important passage such as this...

"For I would not, brethren, that ye should be ignorant of this mystery, lest ye should be wise in your own conceits; that blindness in part is happened to Israel, until the fulness of the Gentiles be come in. And so all Israel shall be saved: as it is written, There shall come out of Sion the Deliverer, and shall turn away ungodliness from Jacob: For this [is] my covenant unto them, when I shall take away their sins. As concerning the gospel, [they are] enemies for your sakes: but as touching the election, [they are] beloved for the fathers' sakes. For the gifts and calling of God [are] without repentance. For as ye in times past have not believed God, yet have now obtained mercy through their unbelief: Even so have these also now not believed, that through your mercy they also may obtain mercy. For God hath concluded them all in unbelief, that he might have mercy upon all. O the depth of the riches both of the wisdom and knowledge of God! how unsearchable [are] his judgments, and his ways past finding out!" Romans 11:25-33

THE FEAST OF TABERNACLES

The Lord God almighty delivered Israelites from the bondage of slavery under Pharaoh and told them to celebrate seven festivals. The Lord spoke to Moses and said to him to proclaim to Israelites those seven festivals and that the festivals should be celebrated on the appointed days. The details of the seven festivals are recorded in Leviticus Chapter 23.

There is resemblance in celebrating "The Festival of Tabernacles" and "Lord's Supper". The "Festival of Tabernacles" is celebrated by the children of Israel to remember their deliverance from the bondage under Pharaoh and the "Lord 's Supper" is celebrated by New Testament believers to remember the death of Lord Jesus Christ who gave His life to redeem man from the bondage of Sin. Israelites are asked to celebrate "The Festival of Tabernacles" and the Lord asked New Testament believers to take part in the "Lord's Supper" to remember Him.

The Lord asked the children of Israel to remember his mercy in delivering them from slavery. This is shadow of the things to come in future. That was fulfilled in Lord Jesus Christ who became our Passover lamb and was crucified for our sake. He died and was buried. Jesus rose from the dead on the third day and after forty days he ascended into heaven.

Before Jesus ascended into heaven he said to his disciples that they should eat and drink from the cup the emblems representing his body and blood in remembrance of his sacrifice on the cross for our sake. The children of Israel have celebrated these festivals and will also celebrate this 'feast of the tabernacles' in future in the Millennium. The nations will also participate in this celebration.

THE DELIVERANCE

"Then the LORD said unto Moses, Now shalt thou see what I will do to Pharaoh: for with a strong hand shall he let them go, and with a strong hand shall he drive them out of his land". (Exodus 6:1)

The LORD delivered the children of Israel with a mighty hand from the bondage of slavery under Pharaoh and led them through wilderness for forty years until they reached Canaan.

The ten plagues that Pharaoh and his people went through for refusing to let the children of Israel go were so unbearable and miserable that Pharaoh finally drove out the children of Israel with a strong hand. Pharaoh did not want the children of Israel any more in Egypt. But soon after Israelites started moving out Pharaoh went after them to get them back again into Egypt but he failed. Pharaoh and his armies were drowned in the Red Sea.

THE PROTECTION

The first instance of the protection the LORD granted to the children of Israel was seen when every one of the Israelites from child to the old, and every cattle passed on the dry land in the midst of the Red Sea. The LORD kept Pharaoh's army far from them by standing in between the children of Israel and Pharaoh's army.

"And the LORD went before them by day in a pillar of a cloud, to lead them the way; and by night in a pillar of fire, to give them light; to go by day and night" (Exodus 13:21)

"...The LORD looked unto the host of the Egyptians through the pillar of fire and cloud and troubled the host of the Egyptians." (Exodus 14:24)

Apostle Paul warns Corinthians in 1 Corinthians 10:1-4 that they should not be ignorant of the fact that Israelites who were redeemed by God from slavery were under the cloud, which was not an ordinary one but the very Shekinah glory of God, throughout their journey from Egypt to Canaan. In the very early period of their journey they passed through the sea.

Their passing in the midst of Red represented their baptism. They all ate of the same spiritual meat and they all drank of the same spiritual drink and that spiritual Rock that followed them was Christ. Jesus Christ was accompanied them and was the protector and provider of Israelites in the wilderness while they journeyed on foot from Egypt to Canaan for forty years.

The two sacraments, that is, the Baptism and the communion, that we do in the present age was in the form of shadow in the Old Testament which is fulfilled in Christ when he broke the bread and asked his disciples to eat of it and drink of the cup that signified his death for our sake. When we participate in the Lord's Supper we do remember the Lord's death, burial and resurrection.

The footwear of the children of Israel did not wear until they reached Canaan. Yet, on their journey they murmured several times and angered God. Finally only Joshua and Caleb and the posterity of those started their journey only reached Canaan.

The word of God says in Deuteronomy 29:5 that the children of Israel did not have any shortage either of food, or of clothing or shelter. It was indeed a great miracle that their shoe did not wear or tear on their feet when they trod the hard path in the wilderness.

The path they trod was not of smooth road as we see in our days but was hard road but the one that we see in rural areas. They did not have shopping centers to do shopping nor did they steal their clothing from somebody but God provided them supernaturally their clothing that did not wear or tear or become old on their bodies. God protected them so wonderfully -- what a privileged people they were – what a blessed nation it was! They were a chosen generation.

God protects us, and provides our needs. By grace through faith we are saved and made equal partners with Jews. There is no difference whether we are Jews or Gentiles; we are all one in Christ and we are the body of Christ and He is the head of the Church. How privileged we are that we are called "royal priesthood" and lively stones built up as spiritual house to offer spiritual sacrifices acceptable to God by Jesus Christ1 Peter 2:5,9)

"And I have led you forty years in the wilderness: your clothes are not waxen old upon you, and thy shoe is not waxen old upon thy foot". (Deuteronomy 29:5)

THE PROVISION

The LORD provided them the heavenly bread, which was called, "Manna", and protected them during day by pillar of clouds and during the night by pillar of fire. In the New Testament we see that Jesus is our bread of life. God provided the Israelites sweet water at Marah and led them by providing all that they needed. (Exodus 15:23-25). In the New Testament we see that Jesus provides living water.

The heavenly bread that the children of Israel received was called "Manna" and like coriander seed, white and tasted like wafers made of honey. God always desired from his people that they should remember his works for his people and how he protected them and provided their needs. That is the reason why God said to Moses to fill an "Omer " of Manna for their generations that they see the bread and remember how God led their fathers in the wilderness after delivering them from the bondage of slavery. (Exodus 16:31-34)

We are his people delivered from the bondage of sin when he bore our sins on the cross and washed our sins in his blood. The Lord now desires from us that we remember his death, burial and resurrection by breaking the bread and eating of it and drinking from the cup in the order that he gave to us.

"In the last day, that great day of the feast, Jesus stood and cried, saying, If any man thirst, let him come unto me, and drink. He that believeth on me, as the scripture hath said, out of his belly shall flow rivers of living water" (John 7:37-38)

Truly the Scripture has said it so in the Old Testament in Isaiah 58:11 (Cf. Isaiah 41:17-18, Isaiah 44:3-4, Joel 3:18)

" And the LORD shall guide thee continually, and satisfy thy soul in drought, and make fat thy bones: and thou shalt be like a watered garden, and like a spring of water, whose waters fail not".

It is about the outpouring of the Holy Spirit on those who are thirsty for Him. God remembered Israelites who were willing to come to him after hearing the warnings. God promised them the blessings. Without the Spirit of God man can not be successful in anything. All things are possible with him and those who depend upon will be successful in their lives. Jesus said he will give his peace to us and not as the world gives and he has also promised before ascension that he will send the Promise of the Father (Luke 24:49).

As Jesus promised Holy Spirit came upon his disciples who were waiting for Him. Later, as Jesus told them they proclaimed the gospel of Jesus Christ, first in Jerusalem, next in Judea and Samaria and then to the uttermost part of the earth. All those whose sins are forgiven are baptized in the Holy Spirit and He indwells them instantly. Is it applicable only to disciples who were waiting at Jerusalem? No! it is applicable to us as well. What with the commission given to the disciples of Jesus that they should preach to every nation -- is it applicable only to them -- No! It is applicable to us as well! Obstructionists do very little for the proclamation of the Gospel of Jesus Christ; instead they delve too deep only to misinterpret the solemn scriptures and say that there is no commission now!

THE LORD DELIVERED THEM

On their way to Canaan, the children of Israel promised to obey the commandments given by God but they failed to keep them several times. The LORD was kind to them throughout their journey by providing them the heavenly bread and water, and protecting them from sun and darkness. On their journey to Canaan they dwelt in tabernacles, also called booths. The LORD God also came and dwelt among them but in the Tabernacle that God asked them to make according to His specifications.

It is amazing to know how the Almighty God came down from his highest abode to dwell among the children of Israel and provided their needs and accepted their worship. The same God came down in incarnation in the form of man and dwelt among men, yet men did not know. After delivering the children of Israel from the bondage of slavery the LORD spoke to Moses saying:

"And the LORD spake unto Moses, saying, Speak unto the children of Israel, saying, In the seventh month, in the first day of the month, shall ye have a sabbath, a memorial of blowing of trumpets, an holy convocation. Ye shall do no servile work therein: but ye shall offer an offering made by fire unto the LORD." (Leviticus 23:23-25)

The Gospel of John speaks undeniable truths:

In the beginning was the Word, and the Word was with God, and the Word was God. (John 1:1)

" ... And the Word was made flesh, and dwelt among us, and we beheld his glory, the glory as of the only begotten of the Father, full of grace and truth "(John 1:14)

"For God so loved the world, that he gave his only begotten Son, that whosoever believeth in him should not perish, but have everlasting life." (John 3:16)

Jesus saith unto him, I am the way, the truth, and the life: no man cometh unto the Father, but by me. (John 14:6)

John was the forerunner and witness of Jesus Christ. He gave testimony of Jesus. John said he was baptizing with water but one that comes after him but preferred before him, whose shoe's latchet he did not deserve to unloose, will baptize with Holy Spirit and with fire.

All those whose sins are forgiven by Jesus will be baptized with Holy Spirit and all those who did not repent will be baptized with fire, which is the lake of fire. (Matthew 3:11). John goes further and introduced Jesus as the "Lamb of God" who takes away the sin of the world. John said that Jesus was before he was. (John 1:26-30)

THE FUTURE

The children of Israel will celebrate this "feast of tabernacles" in the "Millennium". Not only the children of Israel but all the nations will celebrate this festival as the word of God says in Zechariah 14:16-21

Zachariah prophesies about the future Jerusalem which will be for the first time a place of peace. Instead of nations rising against for war the nations will come and worship the King. The thousand year rule of King Jesus will be peaceful as was never seen before in the world history. It will be the time when Jews will celebrate the 'feast of the tabernacles' remembering their forefathers who dwelt in booths while they were on their journey from Egypt to Canaan. God came and dwelt among them.

In the millennium Jesus will be the King over united Israel. The House of Israel and the House of Judah will be united and one as was before king Solomon and even better than that inasmuch as there was none other time where such peace exited as it would exit in the millennium under the rule of Jesus Christ.

"And it shall come to pass, that every one that is left of all the nations which came against Jerusalem shall even go up from year to year to worship the King, the LORD of hosts, and to keep the feast of tabernacles"(Zechariah 14:16)

Luke was detail oriented Physician who differentiates here from the first cup and the second cup. Jesus desired to eat the Passover with his disciples before he suffered at the cross. The Lord gave the first cup to his disciples and asked them to divide among them signifying Passover festival (Luke 22:17). He said he will not drink the fruit of the vine any more until the kingdom of the God shall come in future, and later he took bread and gave thanks and broke it saying

"This is my body which is given for you: this do in remembrance of me" (Luke 22:19).

It was not the Passover festival that we are asked to remember but it is the death of Jesus who became Passover lamb for our sake that we are asked to remember. It is the custom among Jews that during the feast of Passover they sup from four cups. The description of one cup of Passover feast is given first and Jesus said he will sup from this cup in the Kingdom of heaven which is the Kingdom of the Son, in the thousand year reign, when he rules literally from the throne of David. By that time the scattered ten tribes from northern kingdom of Israel and southern kingdom would have been united by the Lord as prophesied. That was the 'New Covenant' prophesied in Jeremiah, which will be fulfilled in the "kingdom of heaven". It is the second cup that Jesus gave to his disciples that represents his blood shed for us.

As the Jews refused to accept Jesus as 'Messiah' the Gentiles had the privilege to enter into His presence. We did not become partakers of the covenant to become one with the House of Israel and/or House of Judah, but we have become partakers of the New Covenant to become the members of His body.

The Church is the bride of Christ, and those who have accepted Jesus as their personal Savior constitute the bride of Christ and in this Church there is no difference between the Jew and Gentile. "For there is no difference between the Jew and the Greek: for the same Lord over all is rich unto all that call upon him. For whosoever shall call upon the name of the Lord shall be saved". (Jeremiah 31:31,Hebrews 8:8, Romans 10:12-13, 1 Corinthians 11:23-26).

We, who are born again and redeemed by the precious blood of Jesus and not with silver or gold, should remember him, who is our savior.

"Being born again, not of corruptible seed, but of incorruptible, by the word of God, which liveth and abideth for ever " (1 Peter 1:23)

The LORD told Moses to proclaim the feasts of the LORD that they may celebrate and not forget Him.

"That your generations may know that I made the children of Israel to dwell in booths, when I brought them out of the land of Egypt: I am the LORD your God". (Leviticus 23:43)

THE REMEMBRANCE

"And the LORD spake unto Moses, saying, Speak unto the children of Israel, saying, The fifteenth day of this seventh month shall be the feast of tabernacles for seven days unto the LORD". (Leviticus 23:33-34)

The LORD asked the children of Israel to celebrate the 'feast of tabernacles' to remember the LORD's compassion, his protection and his provision to the children of Israel. The LORD said to them that they should dwell in booths during the period of this festival. This festival is celebrated that they and their children may recollect how God redeemed them from the bondage of slavery with his mighty hand and led them through the wilderness for forty years providing them food, clothing and shelter.

Not only he provided them their needs but God came and dwelt among them. The feast of tabernacles was to start on fifteenth day of seventh month and should last for seven days. It shall be unto the LORD. On the first day of the festival it shall be an holy convocation and similarly on the eighth day of the festival it shall be an holy convocation. The children of Israel were asked to offer an offering made by fire unto the LORD and they were not supposed to do any servile work therein. (Leviticus 23:33-42).

Now is the time of Remembrance

In the New Testament we see Jesus accepting worship as we read in Gospels. Jesus said He and the Father are one.

"And the multitudes that went before, and that followed, cried, saying, Hosanna to the Son of David: Blessed is he that cometh in the name of the Lord; Hosanna in the highest" Matthew 21:9

A New Testament believer does not need to keep Sabbath. Jesus is our mediator on whose death the veil in the temple was rent from top to bottom indicating that the New Testament believer is free from the stringent laws of the Old Testament laws. Jesus pointed that David, when hungered entered the house of God and ate the showbread which could be eaten only by the priests. Jesus is the Lord of the Sabbath. (Matthew 12:1-8)

Apostle Paul wrote in Colossians 2:16-17 that no man should judge us in meat, or in drink or in respect of an holy day or of the new moon of the Sabbath days.

There are two commandments from Jesus that a New Testament believer has to keep and they are recorded in Mark 12:30-31 – Love thy God with all your heart and with all your soul and with all your strength and the second one is to love your neighbor as yourself.

Jesus said that his death, burial and resurrection should be remembered as often as possible.

"Then Jesus said unto them, Verily, verily, I say unto you, Except ye eat the flesh of the Son of man, and drink his blood, ye have no life in you"(John 6:53)

THE TESTIMONY OF JESUS IS
THE SPIRIT OF PROPHECY

"Therefore doth my Father love me, because I lay down my life, that I might take it again. No man taketh it from me, but I lay it down of myself. I have power to lay it down, and I have power to take it again. This commandment have I received of my Father" (John 10:17-18)

Although the names of the two are not revealed it is evident from the context that these two were disciples of Lord Jesus Christ. One of the disciples was Cleopatus and another is believed by some as Peter and some as Luke. As they walked down the road on the day of resurrection of Lord Jesus in a village called Emmaus they communed with each other about the trial of Jesus, His crucifixion, His death and burial. As they reasoned about these things that happened in Jerusalem Jesus came near them and walked with them. He inquired them of what things they were talking about. Even though they were the disciples of Lord Jesus Christ and saw resurrected Jesus with them they did not recognize Him.

Cleopas answered and asked Jesus a counter question if He was stranger in that land! His question was to ask how that He did not know the recent burning issues that have just happened three days ago. Jesus asked Cleopas as to what things have happened there. The question from Jesus was not because He did not know what has happened recently there but to get more information about their knowledge about the things that have come to pass. Surprisingly, Cleopas gave reply that the things he was talking about were about Jesus of Nazareth who was a prophet mighty in deeds and word before God and all the people.

Jesus said the Father loves Him because He lays down His life that He might take it again. No one can take His life from Him, but He lays it down of Himself and He has the power to lay it down and He has the power to take it again.

Cleopas said that Jesus was to restore the kingdom to Israel and redeem them but the chief Priests and the rulers delivered Jesus to be condemned to death and have crucified Him. He also said that it was the third day after these things have happened. He also explained to Jesus how that certain women went to sepulcher that morning and astonished not finding the body of Jesus in the open sepulcher. The women went out then to give testimony how that the angels told them that Jesus was alive but they did not see Him.

Lord Jesus Christ said to them:

"...O fools, and slow of heart to believe all that the prophets have spoken: Ought not Christ to have suffered these things, and to enter into his glory? And beginning at Moses and all the prophets, he expounded unto them in all the scriptures the things concerning himself" (Luke 24:25-27)

The Scriptures Lord Jesus was referring to were:

Genesis 3:15; 49:10; Numbers 21:8-9; Deuteronomy 18:15; Isaiah 9:6-7; 53:1-12; Psalm 16:1-11,1-11,1-7; Daniel 9:25-27; Malachi 4:2-6.

In spite of all these they did not recognize Lord Jesus Christ and as they were nearing the village He made as though He would have gone further, but they constrained Him to stay with them because it was already evening. Lord Jesus Christ accepted their invitation and stayed with them and as they sat for evening meal He took bread and blessed it, and broke it and gave to them. It was then that their eyes were opened and Lord Jesus Christ vanished from that place.

The two disciples discerned then that the one who spoke to them all the while on the road and sat with them for evening meal was Lord Jesus Christ. They believed that Lord Jesus Christ rose from the dead and gave testimony about Him. (cf. Luke 24:13-15)

Lord Jesus Christ was recognized only when He revealed Himself and when He broke the bread and gave it them to eat. They believed and stood to testify Him.

"And I fell at his feet to worship him. And he said unto me, See thou do it not: I am thy fellow-servant, and of thy brethren that have the testimony of Jesus: worship God: for the testimony of Jesus is the spirit of prophecy" (Revelation 19:10)

JEREMIAH ENCOURAGES

"There is none like unto thee, Jehovah; thou art great, and thy name is great in might" (Jeremiah 10:6)

After the house of Israel was carried away captive Jeremiah the prophet cautions them to pay heed unto the words of Jehovah that they should be careful not to worship idols made of men.

The warning from Jehovah was that they should not learn the ways of nations or be afraid of the written enactments of those nations. God warned them they should not allow their courage to be destroyed by fear when they see the signs of their astrology of heavens. (Jeremiah 10:1)

The Lord said that he was mighty to deliver them from any fear and captivity. Speaking of the mighty power of Jehovah, Solomon the king said that no wisdom, nor any understanding, or counsel against Jehovah will stand. He also said that the mighty warriors may prepare horses for battle but the safety is entirely in the hands of Jehovah. (Proverbs 21:30-31)

Here is the rock of our refuge, the Almighty God, who takes care of us. The believers can boldly say that God takes care of them. The Church consisting of believers is protected and its safety is in the hands of the living God. The assurance is so great that no weapon that is formed against a saint will prosper and the saint's righteousness is of the Lord. Therefore, he shall condemn in judgment every tongue that rises against his saints. (Isaiah 54:17)

God laid few conditions to the children of Israel to follow. They are told by the prophet that the people in those nations make idols from the wood cut from tree out of the forest, work it with chisel, and deck it with silver and with gold. He says that these idols neither speak nor move out from the place where they are placed. He says that they are carried by humans from one place to another.

The children of Israel are advised not to be afraid of those idols because they can neither do any good nor any harm. (Jeremiah 10:4) Psalmist also says that they have mouth but cannot speak: they have eyes, but can not see. (Psalms 115:5) Psalmist says that before the mountains were brought forth, our God created heavens and earth and he was and is and he will be forever. (Psalm 90:2)

Jeremiah continues to encourage them with the words of confidence that there is none like our living God. Among all wise of the nations, there is none like unto our living God. John says in Revelation 15:4 that the Lord is holy and all the nations shall come unto him and pay homage before him.

Men may persecute the children of God but here is the God but nothing takes place in any body's life without his knowledge and permission. Everything works for good for a believer in Christ and every good work for him is accounted for. There is none like our great God, who is powerful to take care of us.

"Come unto me, all ye that labour and are heavy laden, and I will give you rest" (Matthew 11:28)

CHAPTER 3
JOHN SAW THE THRONE OF GOD

It was a great privilege for Apostle John to see the vision of the throne of God. The throne of God was described in its minutest detail in Revelation Chapter 4. We read about the vision that John saw about the One who was seated on the throne and the way he was; and will be worshipped in heaven.

The Word of God says, "he that has eyes let him see; he that has ears let him hear; he that understands let him understand." Prophet Isaiah described the throne of God and the angels guarding it. Prophet Ezekiel described in a closer way; nevertheless John is the one who saw the throne of God to the minutest detail.

As the prophets Isaiah and Ezekiel entered to serve the LORD, they were permitted by HIM to have visions to see the Almighty One. (Isaiah 6:1-13 and Ezekiel 1:1-28).

John's vision was quite distinct from that of the ones which Isaiah and Ezekiel saw. John's vision was about the way God was worshipped; and is being; and will be worshipped. As John looked a door opened and he was invited. John was invited to have a look at the heaven. Until the door was opened the throne and that which was in heaven was not known to John. He was not to make presumptions but to write exactly what he saw.

It was decisively shown by the Almighty God as to what is now and will come to pass in future. He heard a voice calling him to witness the things that will come to pass in future. The voice that called him was like a trumpet and the voice said to him "Come up hither, and I will shew thee things which must be hereafter". There he saw in vision the things that are and the things that will come to pass in the future. As soon as he heard this voice he was taken in spirit and behold, he saw the throne that was set in heaven. He saw the ONE who was seated on the throne. John did not write that he was caught up in to heaven, but he wrote that he was caught up in sprit to witness these things that were as of then, and will come to pass in future. He was still in the island of Patmos.

The vision that he saw appeared to him as real. It is noteworthy that John did not give any name of the One who was seated on the throne. There is, therefore, no scope for anyone to make an idol of how God looks like. The description as John saw was great; to him the One who was seated on the throne appeared like the one in royal robes similar to a prince decked with expensive stones. He appeared like transparent Jasper that offers to the human eye vivid colors in perfection signifying God's glory. He appeared like Sardis that signifies justice of God.

The image of the heaven, the throne and the One, who was seated on the throne were so excellent that John went on describing that there was a rainbow around the throne. It presented a picture of indescribable beauty.

The sight was similar to that of an emerald. The rainbow is a picture of peace as was first presented by God during Noah's time. It was a sign of peace after the cessation of floods during Noah's period. God promised that he will not destroy man any more with flood.

There were twenty four elders sitting in their seats around the throne. On the throne was seated the One who was worthy to receive worship. The twenty four elders in their royalty in appearance were seated on their seats. They had crowns on their heads. It gives us the picture that they represented the saints of whole Church/Assembly of Old Testament and New Testament periods. They have also overcome the temptations in the world and received crowns for being loyal to Him. They are seated and their seating indicated that there was in them peace, rest, satisfaction, and honor. It eliminates the possibility of assuming that they were literal twenty four elders in number around the throne. These twenty four elders, who were clothed in white robes, signified purity. They were saved and their salvation entitled them such a position as they were in. They were imputed with the righteousness of Lord Jesus. They had crowns on their heads. It signifies that they received honor and rewards. They represented the Church on the earth and the exalted place of the victorious Church in heaven.

 From out of the throne proceeded the lightening and thundering and voices and before the throne were seven lamps of fire burning that were of seven Spirits of God. Before the throne was a sea of glass that appeared like a crystal and in the midst of the throne and around the throne there were four beasts that had eyes before and behind full on their bodies.

There were four beasts, which were living creatures near God. They were between God and the twenty four elders. These living creatures are cherubim.

 The first beast looked like lion, the second like a calf, the third had a face of man, and the fourth beast was like a flying eagle These four beasts had each of them six wings around him and they were full of eyes. They did not cease worshipping God saying, 'Holy, holy, holy, Lord God Almighty, which was, and is, and is to come'.

The most accepted interpretation is that the Lion represents nobility, Ox represents strength, human face represents wisdom, and the flying eagle represents swiftness. The beasts worship God that there was none like him. There was none like him before; nor is now, and nor will be in future.

The twenty four elders fall down before God laying down their crowns. They lay down their crowns before him acknowledging that it was by His grace that they have their crowns. They worship him saying, " Thou art worthy, O Lord, to receive glory and honour and power: for thou hast created all things, and for thy pleasure they are and were created".

CHAPPTER 4
THE TRUE TEACHINGS

GOD

"God is a Spirit: and they that worship him must worship him in spirit and in truth" (John 4:24)

God is Trinity, the "Father", the "Son", and "the Holy Spirit". They co-exist, they are co-equal, and though their functions are different, yet they are One God and not three Gods. Jesus Christ is the "Son of God" and he is the creator. Jesus Christ, the Son of God, the very God Himself, came to this world to redeem mankind from the bondage of sin. Jesus Christ, who had two natures, one of divine and another of human, during his ministry on this earth, was the incarnation of the very living God.

Adam was created by God and had no human father, so also Jesus Christ, who was born of the Virgin Mary, had no human father. Jesus Christ was born of the Virgin Mary through the works of the Holy Spirit. John 1:1 In the beginning was the Word, and the Word was with God, and the Word was God. "For there are three that bear witness in heaven, the Father, the Word, and the Holy Spirit: and these three are one".1 John 5:7

THE SON OF GOD

"No man hath seen God at any time; the only begotten Son, which is in the bosom of the Father, he hath declared

him" (John 1:18)

Colossians 1:15-16 Who is the image of the invisible God, the firstborn of all creation: For by him were all things created, that are in heaven, and that are in earth, visible and invisible, whether they be thrones, or dominions, or principalities, or powers: all things were created by him, and for him: Jesus Christ is the image of the invisible God, and he is the creator of this universe and everything in it, and God the Father, the Son, and the Holy Spirit have jointly created man in their own image.

WORD OF GOD

John 1:1 In the beginning was the Word, and the Word was with God, and the Word was God. The Word of God is eternal and is given to us for correction, reproof, and edification. It contains history, but it is not a past history in itself. It is given for all generations for all the time. 2 Timothy 3:16 "All scripture is given by inspiration of God, and is profitable for doctrine, for reproof, for correction, for instruction in righteousness".

MAN'S CREATION

After creating heaven, earth, light, and separating light from darkness, he created sun, moon and the Galaxy, animals and on the sixth day, God created man in their own image and in their own likeness and allowed man to have dominion on every creation and creature. Genesis 1:26 And God said, Let us make man in our image, after our likeness: and let them have dominion over the fish of the sea, and over the fowl of the air, and over the cattle, and over all the earth, and over every creeping thing that creeps upon the earth. On the seventh day

God rested. God made a garden out of the earth and put man in the garden, which he called as "garden of Eden". God told man that he can eat any fruit from the tree in the garden except for eating from the 'tree of the knowledge of the good and evil.'

MAN'S FALL

Adam sinned by disobeying God's command by eating the forbidden fruit brought by his wife EVE, who was deceived by Satan. Adam not only brought the condemnation of death on himself but he passed this sin to all the generations born after him.

The only remission of this sin was by atonement, which was done by our Lord Jesus Christ. Adam and Eve were sent out of the "Garden of Eden" as a consequence of their disobedience to God's Word and lost the spiritual image of God.

Thus death entered the world and it ruled. Man needed a Savior to be clothed with the righteousness and holiness of God. Therefore, God sent in to this world, His one and only begotten son, Jesus Christ, who is the exact representation of God the Father and is God Himself. He came in flesh in to this world to redeem us from sin and when He was on this earth He had two natures, one of divine and another of human.

ATONEMENT OF SINS

"For God so loved the world that he gave his only begotten Son, that whosoever believeth in him should not perish, but have everlasting life". John 3:16 "All things are delivered unto me of my Father: and no man knoweth the Son, but the Father;

neither knoweth any man the Father, save the Son, and he to whomsoever the Son will reveal him". Matthew 11:27

"For when we were yet without strength, in due time Christ died for the ungodly." Romans 5:6

"For to this end Christ both died, and rose, and revived, that he might be Lord both of the dead and living." Romans 14:9

"For I delivered unto you first of all that which I also received, how that Christ died for our sins according to the scriptures;" 1 Corinthians 15:3

"For to this end Christ both died, and rose, and revived, that he might be Lord both of the dead and living." Romans 14:9

Jesus Christ came down to this world, died for our sake bearing our sins upon the cross of Calvary. He was buried, rose from the dead on the third day, and ascended in to heaven.

SALVATION

Salvation cannot be earned by any type of goods works or sacrifices of animals nor can it be purchased by gold or silver or any precious element. Salvation is available free of cost for all those who believe in Lord Jesus Christ, confess his/her sins to him and acknowledge HIM as his/her personal Savior.

"If we confess our sins, he is faithful and just to forgive us our sins, and to cleanse us from all unrighteousness."1 John 1:9.

Those who receive Jesus Christ as their personal savior will become his children.

"But as many as received him, to them gave he power to become the children of God, even to them that believe on his name:" John 1:12.

Whoever believes in him shall not perish but have eternal life. We cannot receive salvation unless we ask for it from God. The salvation, which we receive by accepting Jesus Christ as our personal savior cannot be lost. Lord Jesus Christ paid the price for our salvation by shedding his precious blood upon the cross of Calvary and redeemed us. He finished all the works for us leaving for us only the requirement of believing in him, and accepting him with faith as the Lord. Believing in heart and confessing sins to him and acknowledging with mouth that HE is the Lord, is all that is required. He is faithful to preserve us from falling and restore us if we backslide.

DARKNESS IN DAY TIME

Eli, Eli, lama sabachthani?
(My God, my God, why hast thou forsaken me?)

From Matthew 27:46

"Now from the sixth hour there was darkness over all the land unto the ninth hour. And about the ninth hour Jesus cried with a loud voice, saying, Eli, Eli, lama sabachthani? that is to say, My God, my God, why hast thou forsaken me?" (Matthew 27:45-46)

From the sixth hour of the day in Jerusalem until the ninth of hour there, which is equivalent to 12.00 PM to 3.00 PM of our time, there was utter darkness on the face of the earth when Jesus was on the cross, bearing our sin upon Himself.

It pleased the Father to bruise His Son Jesus for our sin (cf. prophecy in Isaiah 53:10), and our sin was judged at the cross by the righteous Lord God.

"Yet it pleased the LORD to bruise him; he hath put him to grief: when thou shalt make his soul an offering for sin, he shall see his seed, he shall prolong his days, and the pleasure of the LORD shall prosper in his hand" (Isaiah 53:10)

It was at that time that the Father brought about severest darkness on the face of the earth. Jesus took our punishment on Himself and our sin on Him was judged at the Cross. The Father, the Holy One, could not see the sin on the Son Jesus Christ, and that is the reason why the Father judged the sin at the cross where Lord Jesus was hung bearing our sin. Darkness signifies judgment and during this darkness our sin was judged at the Cross.

"For he hath made him to be sin for us, who knew no sin; that we might be made the righteousness of God in him" (2 Corinthians 5:21)

"Christ hath redeemed us from the curse of the law, being made a curse for us: for it is written, Cursed is every one that hangeth on a tree" (Galatians 3:13)

"his body shall not remain all night on the tree, but you shall bury him the same day, for a hanged man is cursed by God. You shall not defile your land that the LORD your God is giving you for an inheritance" (Deuteronomy 21:23 ESV)

Jesus, who knew no sin, was made sin for us in order that we might be made the righteousness of God in Him. There are contentious beliefs that Father can look upon the sin of man, and therefore, Jesus was not forsaken; but considering the fact that sin is pernicious, heinous, offensive and polluted, it is hardly believable that the Holy Father God could see sin upon the Son of God.

In the Old Testament according to the Law, Moses was commanded by the LORD, to burn the bullock, and his hide, his flesh and his dung outside the camp. This shadow was fulfilled in Jesus when the sin on Him was judged at Golgotha, outside the city, in order that He may become propitiation and die a substitutionary death on behalf of us to redeem us to give us everlasting life. Anyone can receive this everlasting life by believing that Jesus is the Lord and God raised Him from the dead.

"But the bullock, and his hide, his flesh, and his dung, he burnt with fire without the camp; as the LORD commanded Moses" (Leviticus 8:17)

It was neither an eclipse nor was the usual darkness that came at sunset, but it was utter darkness from noon to three past noon. It was during the Passover that this darkness came upon the face of the earth and this darkness prevailed on the face of the earth in the midst of the day light. It was indeed unusual.

"Verily, verily, I say unto you, He that heareth my word, and believeth on him that sent me, hath everlasting life, and shall not come into condemnation; but is passed from death unto life". (John 5:24)

Darkness was one of the ten plagues that God brought on Egypt. "And the LORD said unto Moses, Stretch out thine hand toward heaven, that there may be darkness over the land of Egypt, even darkness [which] may be felt. And Moses stretched forth his hand toward heaven; and there was a thick darkness in all the land of Egypt three days" Exodus 10:21,22

"And it came between the camp of the Egyptians and the camp of Israel; and it was a cloud and darkness to them, but it gave light by night to these: so that the one came not near the other all the night". (Exodus 14:20)

Darkness is accompanied with fear, sin, and judgment. It is opposed to luster and honor. It is opposed to wisdom; it is associated with confusion, folly, vexation of Spirit, and calamities. An angel shone light towards Israelites when Israelites were just about to cross Red Sea, and darkness to Pharaoh and his army. It was the judgment that Pharaoh and his army were about to face while the children of God were about to cross the Red Sea.

Scriptures speak of the sun and the moon getting fully darkened, and the stars withdrawing their shining in the last days. It happens when the Lord comes again to this earth.

"The sun and the moon shall be darkened, and the stars shall withdraw their shining". (Joel 3:15)

When Jesus was on the cross he quoted directly from Psalm 22:1 and cried aloud "Eli, Eli, lama sabachthani? that is to say, My God, my God, why hast thou forsaken me?"

"My God, my God, why hast thou forsaken me? why art thou so far from helping me, and from the words of my roaring?" (Psalms 22:1)

Although the details of separation or non-separation of the Father and the Son at the cross, for a while, are known to the Father and the Son only, yet it is worth considering, to the best of our knowledge, whether or not the Son was forsaken at the Lord's death and why Lord Jesus said "My God, my God, why hast thou forsaken me?" It is necessary that we understand what exactly happened during those dark hours, and the way the Father judged sin upon the Son.

Lord Jesus had two natures in His incarnation when He relinquished His glory that He had with the Father and came into this world in the form of a servant and in the likeness of man.

One nature that He had was of divine and the other of human. He felt the human traits such as joy, pain, sadness, hunger. He wept at the tomb of Lazarus, who was dead for four days. However, the pain He suffered at the cross was, indeed, much more in its intensity. He bore our sin and took the penalty of our sin upon Himself and paid for our sin and punishment. It was not by silver or by gold that we were redeemed but by His precious blood, and therefore, the cost of our redemption was very heavy.

Lord Jesus felt separation from the Father just as the David felt separation from God but the Lord was not forsaken to be our savior or ceased to be God. He was for a short while, in His human nature, felt all alone while our sin was on Him. God is Almighty, who is triune, and who lives forever and ever, is inseparable. God is omnipresent, omniscient, and omnipotent.

"Thus saith the LORD, The heaven is my throne, and the earth is my footstool: where is the house that ye build unto me? and where is the place of my rest?" (Isaiah 66:1)

It would also be apt to consider here whether or not David felt separation from God when He cried "My God, my God, why hast thou forsaken me? why art thou so far from helping me, and from the words of my roaring?" (Psalms 22:1)

The caption of the Psalm is "To the chief Musician upon Aijeleth Shahar, A Psalm of David" David was singing a song extemporarily, an unknown tune, pointing to Lord Jesus Christ's sufferings than to himself. It was an unknown future to him. When He sang the song He neither felt Jesus would be separated from the Father or not but He said "My God, my God why hast thou forsaken me" in prophecy. The psalm is Messianic. He did not mean Jesus would be separated or would not be separated; however the word meaning of "forsaken" is abandon.

David lost fellowship with God when He had illegal relationship with Bathsheba and got her husband Uriah killed. His sin did not go unpunished. God dealt with Him severely but taking away his firstborn son, and putting him to terrible ignominy (Ref. 2 Samuel 12:1-19).

Similarly when Jesus was on the cross He, in His human nature was bearing our sin and that sin was judged severely by the Father and Jesus felt separation from the Father; however God raised Him from the dead and said to Him "You are my Son, today I have begotten you".

So also Christ did not exalt himself to be made a high priest, but was appointed by him who said to him, "You are my Son, today I have begotten you"; (Hebrews 5:5 ESV)

Psalmist goes on singing the song indicating the Lord's exaltation in His future kingdom. He concludes the psalm in praises and the Lord's exaltation as the King.

"All the prosperous of the earth eat and worship; before him shall bow all who go down to the dust, even the one who could not keep himself alive. Posterity shall serve him; it shall be told of the Lord to the coming generation; they shall come and proclaim his righteousness to a people yet unborn, that he has done it" (Psalm 22:29-31 ESV)

Lord Jesus said:

 "I and my Father are one". (John 10:30)

Although the word "forsaken" in Hebrew, Greek and in English means "abandon" Lord Jesus Christ was not forsaken eternally, but He felt separation from the Father, because He was bearing our sin upon Himself, and that is why He was quoting from Psalm 22:1 when He cried "My God, my God, why hast thou forsaken me?"

"And about the ninth hour Jesus cried with a loud voice, saying, Eli, Eli, lama sabachthani? that is to say, My God, my God, why hast thou forsaken me?" (Matthew 27:46)

Let us worship the Father in the name of our Lord and Savior Jesus Christ, who was crucified, died for our sake, was buried and was raised from the dead on the third day. Jesus ascended into heaven and he is seated on the right hand of the Majesty.

SCAPEGOAT

"Because the Tabernacle remained in the midst of the children of Israel with all their transgressions and uncleanness, Aaron, the high priest makes atonement for the holy place. He brings the live goat and lays both his hands upon the head of the live goat, signifying the transference of the sins of himself, and all the people of Israel on to the live goat, and confesses over the live goat all the iniquities of the children of Israel, and all the transgressions and all their sins, and sends it away by the hand of the fit man into the wilderness. The goat carries the iniquities of all the people of Israel unto a land not inhabited never to return again to the land where the children of Israel lived. The live goat on which the sins are confessed is led outside the camp by a fit man into the wilderness" (Leviticus 16:16-19)

Notice the shedding of the blood and its sprinkling covered their sins, yet the sins remained in the sanctuary until the high priest transferred the sins onto the live goat which carried the sins far into an uninhabited land. The letting of the scapegoat into the wilderness is after the high priest changes his garments of linen and puts on his priestly garments and offering of the fat of the sin offering to be burnt upon the altar (Ref: Leviticus 16:20-22)

THE SCRITPURE SAYS:

"For he hath made him to be sin for us, who knew no sin; that we might be made the righteousness of God in him" (2 Corinthians 5:21)

LORD JESUS CHRIST BECAME SACRIFICE AND HE BORE OUR SIN ON BEHALF OF US

Here is the crux of the problem.   According to belief of some Satan is the originator of sin and, therefore, Satan carries sin into the wilderness never to return. If anyone believes otherwise, they say, he gets mark of the beast and this is false teaching.

SPIRITS

"And every spirit that confesseth not that Jesus Christ is come in the flesh is not of God: and this is that spirit of antichrist, whereof ye have heard that it should come; and even now already is it in the world" (1 John 4:3)

Any spirit that denies the following two verses is not from God, but from evil.

"In the beginning was the Word, and the Word was with God, and the Word was God". John 1:1

"And the Word was made flesh, and dwelt among us, (and we beheld his glory, the glory as of the only begotten of the Father,) full of grace and truth" John 1:14

THE CHURCH/ASSEMBLY

All those who are saved through the blood of Jesus Christ constitute the Church/Assembly and is the future bride of Jesus Christ. Church/Assembly does not mean any denomination or any local body of Church/Assembly but it is the body consisting of all those who are saved through the blood of Jesus Christ.

BODY, SOUL, AND SPIRIT

Man has the BODY, the SOUL, and the SPIRIT. [Man in general includes men and women.] Body is the physical structure of the man, Soul is the immaterial part of a person; the actuating cause of an individual life and the spirit is the breath of life given by God. Body perishes at the death of the person, the saved SOUL will ascend to be with the Lord Jesus Christ in heaven, when the person dies, and the SPIRIT of the saved or the unsaved returns to God. God breathed His spirit in to the nostrils of man when he created him, so the spirit of saved or unsaved will return to God. The saved ones will have eternal life, while the unsaved one will be cast in to hell.

The Soul of the unsaved one will remain in the hell and tormented until the time of final judgment comes and they will be judged in the final judgment and after they are judged, they along with Satan and his fallen angels, death and hell will be cast in to the lake fire. [Rev.19:20, 20:10, 20:14,15] The souls of the saved ones are comforted in Paradise in the third heaven until the time of second coming of Jesus Christ takes place and at the judgment seat of Christ in the mid-air, they receive their rewards for their good works.

HEAVENS

There are three heavens, one from the face of the earth up to the place where clouds are seen, and birds can fly, the second one from the place where the first heaven ends up to the place where galaxy exists, and third heaven, which is the infinite space beyond our imagination is the abode of God.

THE REIGN OF ANTI-CHRIST

Satan is cast down to the earth as a result of the war in heaven that takes place (Revelation Ch.12:7-12) and he is revealed as the "Man of Sin", the Anti-Christ, who makes promises and breaks them and deceives people. Satan also has Trinity consisting of (1) The Dragon (The Anti-God) Rev. 12:1-7 (2) The Beast (Anti-Christ) Rev. 13:1-10 and (3) The False Prophet (Anti-Spirit)Rev.13:11-17. False prophet brings glory to the Anti-Christ, who equals himself with Jesus Christ and will proclaim himself as Jesus Christ and deceive people. Both False prophet and the Anti-Christ work for the Old Dragon, who is the Anti-God.

RESURRECTION

The saints dead shall rise first with their glorious bodies, and the live saints are transitioned with their glorious bodies at the Rapture and will be caught up in to the midair to meet Lord

Jesus Christ. At the Judgment seat of Christ in the Midair the Saints are rewarded for their good works [2 Cor.5:10, Rom 14:16].

The Kingdom of Antichrist will be on the earth at the same time when the Church is with Jesus Christ in the Midair. Anti-Christ's Kingdom lasts up to Millennial Kingdom. [Dan 7:23-27, 2 Thess.2:3-10] The Great Tribulation period is under the reign of Anti-Christ, and runs concurrently when the church is with Jesus Christ in the mid-air. [Rev. 17:1-18]

Lord Jesus Christ along with the Church/Assembly descend on to the earth after the seven year period is over. Lord Jesus Christ reigns from the "Throne of David" for thousand years, which is also commonly known as 'Millennium'. The church will be in heaven during the renovation period of the earth "BY FIRE" [2Pet 3:7-13Rev. 20:11] The church descends in the New Jerusalem on the New Earth.

RAPTURE

"Rapture" is the commonly used word, for what is described in 1 Thessalonians 4:17, which reads as "Then we who are alive and remain shall be caught up together with them in the clouds, to meet the Lord in the air: and so shall we ever be with the Lord". The rapture of the church is before the thousand year reign of Jesus Christ commences. Jesus Christ returns for the second time and the saints are caught up to meet up in the air before the millennium and that is the pre-millennial rapture of the church [1 Thessalonians 4:16-17].

Jesus Christ's second coming will be personal and visible. The saved ones, who died will rise first with their glorious bodies and will be caught up in to the clouds to be with Jesus Christ. Lord Jesus Christ will bring the souls of all the saved ones, who died before his second coming. Jesus Christ brings them along with him and those souls will unite with their bodies in the graves and resurrect and be caught up in to the mid-air with their glorified bodies.

 It will all be instant and will be at the lightning speed. Jesus Christ and the saints will be in the midair for a period of seven years. The church consisting of all the saved ones, will not undergo Tribulation and Great Tribulation, during which period Anti-Christ will be active. [...Read more about pre-tribulation rapture ...]

REMNANT

Those who are left behind on this earth at the time of second coming of Jesus Christ will consist of unsaved Jews and unsaved Gentiles, who will be given opportunity to be saved during the intervening period of the stay of Jesus and saints in the mid-air and his advent on this earth. The Great Tribulation occurs during this period, that is, before the advent of Jesus Christ on this earth to rule for thousand years. Great Tribulation is like "Jacob's Trouble" [Jeremiah 30:7, Matt.24:21, Rev.2:22, Rev.7:14].

The "Man of sin" makes a covenant of peace for one week (seven years) and breaks it in the middle of the week i.e., after three and half years [Dan.9:27]. The next three and half years are filled with great tribulation for those who have not accepted

Lord Jesus Christ as their personal Savior. Then after seven year-period Jesus Christ along with saints will descend to the earth rule for thousand years.

The thousand year reign of Jesus Christ will be peaceful and joyful. An angel with the key of bottomless pit comes down from heaven and lays hold on the hold on the dragon, that old serpent, which is the Devil, and Satan, and binds for a thousand years.

Thus Satan will be bound and will be cast in to bottomless pit and will be shut up during the thousand-year-reign of Jesus Christ. The saints (the church) will also reign along with Jesus Christ during this thousand-year-period. Satan will be released from the bottomless pit after the thousand-year reign of Jesus Christ ends. Satan will, then, go Gog and Magog and will deceive nations and gather people to fight against Jesus Christ and fire comes down from heaven and devours them. Then Satan will be cast in to the lake of fire.

The sea gives up the dead and the death and Hades gives up the dead. Then there is great white throne judgment, where the unsaved ones, whose names are not found in the "book of life" will be judged. The Satan with his fallen angels, the unsaved ones, the death and hell will be cast in to the lake of fire. This is the second death. The new heaven and the new earth, will come down from heaven, where the saved ones will live eternally with the Lord Jesus Christ.

FIRST DEATH AND SECOND DEATH

There is only one death for the saved ones; the unsaved ones will be cast in to lake of fire after the final judgment, and that is their second death, which does not include their loss of life, but includes unbearable sufferings.[Rev.2:11,Rev.20:6,Rev.20:14] Every one born in this will be judged; saved ones for their good works and the unsaved ones for their punishment. Judgments:

1.The judgment at the cross of Calvary for Believers' sins [John 5:24], 2.Judgment of the saints in the midair (at the Judgment seat of Christ) for their works and for their rewards: [2 Cor.5:10],
3.Judgment of the Jews during the Great Tribulation:[Matt.24:20-21], 4.Judgment of the Nations at Jerusalem:[Matt.25:31-32], and after the millennium 5.Judgment of the wicked at the Great White Thorne:[Rev.20:11-12].

In the final judgment, the names of those not found in the "book of life" will be cast into lake of fire. The saved ones will not have second death. The saved ones will have eternal life and the unsaved ones will be in the lake of fire in the outer space, where they will suffer forever. The Satan along with his fallen angels, death and hell will be cast in to lake of fire in to the outer dark space, where they will eternally suffer.

DEAD IN CHRIST SHALL RISE FIRST

"For the Lord himself shall descend from heaven with a shout, with the voice of the archangel, and with the trump of God: and the dead in Christ shall rise first: Then we which are alive and remain shall be caught up together with them in the clouds, to meet the Lord in the air: and so shall we ever be with the Lord" (1 Thessalonians 4:16-17)

'The dead in Christ shall rise first and the living saints shall be caught up together with them in the clouds to meet the Lord in the air'. This blessed hope is given to us that we will be with the Lord forever. The resurrection of the dead with the glorified bodies will be 'in a moment, in the twinkling of an eye at the last trump: for the trumpet shall sound, and the dead shall be raised incorruptible, and we shall be changed' before the commencement of Daniel's Seventieth week, that is 'great tribulation'.

"But every man in his own order: Christ the first-fruits; afterward they that are Christ's at his coming" 1 Corinthians 15:23. There are several reasons to believe that the 'rapture' precedes the 'great tribulation' and that believers in Christ will not see or be part of the 'great tribulation'. Jesus Christ's second coming will be personal and visible. The Lord will descend from heaven with a shout, with the voice of the archangel and with the 'trump of God'.

The Church (Ekklesia) is the precious possession of Lord Jesus Christ and, therefore, it is His love for the Church, and the faithfulness that He has toward His bride that He keeps His bride away from the earthly 'great tribulation', which is primarily for the earthly people and for those, who have rejected Lord Jesus Christ as their Messiah.

 Those, who have accepted Jesus as their personal Savior and Lord, by confessing their sins to Him are the treasured possession of Him, and He protects them from the 'great tribulation, which is meant for the children of Israel, who have rejected as their Messiah.

Two fold purposes of Lord Jesus Christ coming to this earth, is to restore the children of Israel their earthly kingdom, which God had promised to their fathers, and also for the heathen to see God's judgment on those, who sinned and rejected Him as their Savior.

The Church always remains with Him with heavenly blessings showered on them by God and are away from the earthly things. That is the reason why when Lord Jesus Christ descends from heaven in the clouds with a shout, with the voice of archangel, those saints, who are dead in Christ shall rise first and those, who are alive and remain shall be caught up together with them in the clouds, to meet Him in the air, and thereafter we will be with Him forever.

"It is sown a natural body; it is raised a spiritual body. There is a natural body, and there is a spiritual body". (1 Corinthians 15:44)

"In a moment, in the twinkling of an eye, at the last trump: for the trumpet shall sound, and the dead shall be raised incorruptible, and we shall be changed". (1 Corinthians 15:52)";

THE MARRIAGE OF THE LAMB

The church has always been a chaste virgin and the bride of the Lord and will be united in marriage when ruptured at the second coming Jesus Christ in mid and will come down to earth after a period of seven years and literally rule on earth along with Jesus Christ for one thousand years. Revelation 19:7 Let us be glad and rejoice, and give honour to him: for the marriage of the Lamb is come, and his wife hath made herself ready.

NEW HEAVENS AND NEW EARTH

There is clear distinction between those who are saved before the coming of our Lord and Savior Jesus Christ in to the mid-air, where the church, consisting of saints will meet him, and those who are saved during the Great Tribulation period.

Those who are saved before the second coming of our Lord have greater privileges like resurrecting with glorified bodies, meeting him in the air and after a period of seven years coming down on to the earth, reigning with him on the earth for a period of thousand years, spending eternity in the New Heaven.

Those who are saved during the Great Tribulation period do not have as many privileges as those saved before the second coming of our Lord. Those who are saved during the Great Tribulation period will be without glorified bodies and spend their eternity in the New Earth.

When the New Heaven and New Earth are created by Lord Jesus Christ and the saved ones occupy their possessions the Old Earth and Old Heavens will be destroyed.

Isaiah 65:17 "For, behold, I create new heavens and a new earth: and the former shall not be remembered, nor come into mind".

Revelation 21:1 And I saw a new heaven and a new earth: for the first heaven and the first earth were passed away; and there was no more sea.

SECOND COMING OF JESUS IS IMMINENT

The second coming of Lord Jesus is imminent. For a believer, rapture is the second coming of Jesus and for an unbeliever the second appearance of Jesus on the earth is the second coming of Jesus. The end time's prophecies are detailed for us in order that we may have faith and blessed hope of being received by Lord Jesus Christ and be with Him eternally.

The sequence of events leading to the Second coming of Jesus and his establishment of the millennial rule on the earth are disputed among Christians; however the undisputable fact among Christians is that the return of the Lord Jesus Christ and the resurrection of the dead saints from their graves followed by the living saints getting caught up. The doctrine of 'Rapture' of the Church for keeping it away from the 'great tribulation' in the midair for seven years is as disputed as the doctrine of rapture of the Church after the 'great tribulation'.

The word, 'rapture's is not found in the Scriptures; however in essence the meaning of the said word is getting caught up into the air. Lord Jesus Christ's purpose of coming again to this earth is two-fold; firstly the second coming is for receiving His own to Himself and secondly, to fulfill the promises made to Israel.

Church consisting of saved ones constitutes His bride and the marriage of the bride takes place according to Scriptures when the Church is caught up into midair.

To this marriage between the Lord and His bride are not invited the unsaved ones. Lord Jesus Christ promised mansions, which He promised, for his children. He promised that He was going to heaven to prepare mansions for them.

This promise is given in John 14:3 and this purpose, which was a mystery and hidden in the Old Testament, is revealed in the New Testament. Yet, confusion prevails among Christians about the promises that Jesus gave to His children.

The earthly blessings promised to the children of Israel will be restored unto them when Lord Jesus Christ appears on this earth. Jesus rules literally for one thousand years sitting on the throne of David fulfilling prophesies.

The Church consisting of heavenly ones, saved in the precious blood of Lord Jesus Christ is His precious bride for His bride consisting of blessed ones should not be confused with the Israel. The covenants made to the children of Israel will be fulfilled on this earth. Ref: Acts 1:6, Hebrews 9:28, Romans 11:28, etc. Israel and the Church are separate and if this fact is understood clearly much confusion that prevails among Christians about 'rapture' will fade away.[...Read more about pre-tribulation rapture ...]

CHAPER 5
ROYAL PRIESTHOOD

"Ye also, as lively stones, are built up a spiritual house, an holy priesthood, to offer up spiritual sacrifices, acceptable to God by Jesus Christ". (1 Peter 2:5)

The status given to New Testament believers is exceptional and extraordinary. The New Testament believers are lively stones built up to form a spiritual house where the spiritual sacrifices are offered and acceptable to God by Jesus Christ. In contrast to the Old Testament physical sacrifices, we, who are New Testament believers, are a holy priesthood. We are given the privilege to offer the spiritual sacrifices.

We are privileged to worship our God in spirit and in truth, with all our heart, with all our soul and with our all mind. Samaritan woman thought her worship was right, but Jesus had to correct her. Faith in God, services rendered to him, honoring his children with our substance, obedience to God, offering our bodies a living sacrifice, pure thoughts, keeping our bodies holy because it is the temple of God, and loving our neighbors as ourselves, are all spiritual sacrifices.

Before the law was given the head of the each family was the priest of that house, and after the law was given Israel was to have become 'kingdom of priests' through their perfect obedience, but they failed to keep the commandments that resulted in confining the priestly office to the tribe of Levi (Aaron and his family).

The priest could go into the 'holiest of all' only once a year to offer the sacrifice. The law could hold everyone guilty of faltering on one count or the other. The grace and truth came from Lord Jesus Christ, who became the perfect sacrifice for us and entered into the holiest of all, on behalf of us, renting the veil of the temple top to bottom, and giving all the New Testament believers the privilege of offering up spiritual sacrifices through the one and only mediator, the Lord Jesus Christ.

Lord Jesus Christ suffered for us setting an example for us to follow. Christ did no sin, nor was any guile found in his mouth. He did not revile back his enemies who reviled him. He was the Son of God, and yet he did not threaten any mortal even when he was suffering. Rather, he said, "Father, forgive them; for they know not what they do..." (Luke 23:34). He bore our sins in his body and the cross that we being dead to sins may become live unto righteousness. We were all as sheep gone astray but are saved through his precious blood shed on the cross of Calvary. He cried aloud and said "Father, into thy hands I commend my spirit; and having said thus, he gave up the ghost". (Luke 23:46)

"For ye were as sheep going astray; but are now returned unto the Shepherd and Bishop of your souls" (1 Peter 2:1-25)

CHAPTER 6
LIVING SACRIFICE

"I beseech you therefore, brethren, by the mercies of God, that ye present your bodies a living sacrifice, holy, acceptable unto God, which is your reasonable service" (Romans 12:1)

Apostle Paul uses a unique word, 'beseech' while addressing Chief Captain (Acts 21:39), King Agrippa (Acts 26:3), brethren at Rome (Romans 12:1 and 15:30) brethren at Corinthians (1 Cor.1:10), which shows how loving and humble he was in his approach with others. 'Beseech' means to beg anxiously, or to request earnestly.

In this verse Paul requests earnestly his fellow believers at Rome to present their bodies a living sacrifice. What exactly 'living sacrifice' means? In the Old Testament period, the physical sacrifices are made to God to have reconciliation with him by way of 'Atonement' for the sin man had committed.

The sacrifices could be a goat, a lamb, or turtledoves. Inasmuch as Christ became our 'propitiation' (a word used in New Testament in lieu of 'Atonement' of Old Testament), we in this New Testament period are no longer required to offer the physical offerings.

Christ is 'Atonement' and his blood that was shed and sprinkled and his body that bore our sins is enough for salvation. All that an unbeliever has to do is to believe in this fact, confess his/her sins to him and accept him as "Lord". After that we continually offer our bodies as living sacrifice unto God.

The believers in Christ are to show kindness, humbleness of mind, meekness, and longsuffering (Col. 3:12), present bodies as holy temple because the Spirit of God lives in us (1 Corinthians 3:16), and worship him in truth and sprit. This is the reasonable service unto him. The true worship is not a forced one, but of voluntary and emanates from the bottom of heart, offering ourselves fully unto him with complete devotion.

"Know ye not that ye are the temple of God, and that the Spirit of God dwelleth in you?" (1 Corinthians 3:16)

CHAPTER 7 FALSE TEACHINGS

WHO WERE SADDUCEES?

Sadducees were first mentioned in the Bible in connection with John the Baptist's ministry. Those from Jerusalem, Judea and round about Jordan who confessed their sins were baptized by John the Baptist.

"And were baptized of him in Jordan, confessing their sins".
Matthew 3:6

John the Baptist saw Sadducees and said to them

"But when he saw many of the Pharisees and Sadducees come to his baptism, he said unto them, O generation of vipers, who hath warned you to flee from the wrath to come?" Matthew 3:7

Sadducees tempted Jesus and He called them

"A wicked and adulterous generation seeketh after a sign; and there shall no sign be given unto it, but the sign of the prophet Jonas. And he left them, and departed" Matthew 16:4.

Sadducees did not believe in Resurrection nor did they believe in after life, or angels or demons.

"The same day came to him the Sadducees, which say that there is no resurrection, and asked him" Matthew 22:23

"For the Sadducees say that there is no resurrection, nor angel,

nor spirit, but the Pharisees acknowledge them all" Acts 23:8.

They took Peter and John into custody when they were preaching the Gospel and Resurrection:

"And as they spake unto the people, the priests, and the captain of the temple, and the Sadducees, came upon them, Being grieved that they taught the people, and preached through Jesus the resurrection from the dead. Acts 4:1, 2

Jesus said unto her, *"I am the resurrection, and the life: he that believeth in me, though he were dead, yet shall he live"* John 11:25

Even these days there are some who profess that they are Christians and yet they teach that there is no resurrection, no life after death, no angels and no demons. These are false teachers.

MARK OF THE BEAST

There is a false teaching that those who do not observe seventh day a Sabbath and those who do not believe that scape goat symbolizes Satan who carries the sin of mankind will get 'mark of the beast' . It is not so. Those who do not worship 'Antichrist', son of perdition, will get the 'mark of the beast'. It is Lord Jesus Christ who bore the sin of man on Himself and died on the cross, was buried and was raised from the dead with uncorrupted body on the third day and later after forty days He ascended into heaven. Lord Jesus Christ is seated on the right of the Majesty pleading on our behalf and will come soon.

And the smoke of their torment ascendeth up for ever and ever: and they have no rest day nor night, who worship the beast and his image, and whosoever receiveth the mark of his name. (Revelation 14:11)

VICTORY OVER THE BEAST

According to John's vision those who did not worship the beast were victorious and had the harps of GOD

"And I saw as it were a sea of glass mingled with fire: and them that had gotten the victory over the beast, and over his image, and over his mark, and over the number of his name, stand on the sea of glass, having the harps of God" (Revelation 15:2)

FALSE TEACHING

While the teaching says sin offering pointed to Christ as sacrifice, the high priest is presented as mediator and the scapegoat typified Satan. The teaching says Satan is the originator of sin, and therefore, it is on Satan's head are placed the sins confessed. The scapegoat typifying Satan is banished from the presence of God and His people and he will be blotted out in the final destruction of sin and sinners.

In other words the teaching holds Satan as the redeemer of mankind taking upon him the sins of the sinners and getting banished. This is in contradiction to what the Scriptures say. The scriptures say Lord Jesus Christ bore our sins and paid his blood as ransom to deliver mankind from sins and whoever believes in Jesus as Savior and confesses his/her sins to Him, he/she will have everlasting life. Satan will be cast into 'Lake of Fire' along with death and hell.

SHOULD WE KEEP SABBATH?

"Remember the sabbath day, to keep it holy". (Exodus 20:8)

The fourth commandment of the Ten Commandments given to the children of Israel was in controversy for a very long time in the history of Christianity. It was a question as to whether Sabbath needs to be observed or not, and if observed whether it is to be observed on Saturday or on Sunday. There are few facts to be considered while dealing with the Sabbath Command.

- To who was the fourth command (that is to keep Sabbath) was given
- Was the fourth command there in existence before it was given
- What was to be done or not to be done on the day of Sabbath
- What the punishment was if there is disobedience shown to the commandment.

Before we deal with the subject of Sabbath it is essential that we go back to Genesis Chapter 2 where the details about rest are mentioned. Genesis Chapter 2:2-3 read:

"And on the seventh day God ended his work which he had made; and he rested on the seventh day from all his work which he had made. And God blessed the seventh day, and sanctified it: because that in it he had rested from all his work which God created and made".

In Genesis Chapter 1:28-31 the creation account of the sixth day is narrated. On the sixth day God created man in his own image.

He created male and female on the same day although details as to how He created are given in the next chapter.

There are few explicit commands given by God to man; some of them are permissive and one was highly restrictive. The permissive commands were not optional that the man can give up on them nor did the restrictive one was there for him to disobey.

God gave those commands to man to surely obey. God is the creator and He has the authority to give commands. It is not for man to say why God had given such commands to man. Man and the whole creation is God's possession.

God blessed man and woman and said to them to be fruitful, multiply, and replenish the earth and subdue it. God gave authority to them to have dominion over the fish of the sea, over the fowl of the air, and over every living creature that moves on the earth. God gave them every herb bearing seed, every tree which bears fruit that yields seed as meat for them to eat. When the sixth day came to an end the creation was fully done by God and he said everything that he had made was very good.

GOD RESTED ON THE SEVENTH DAY

From Genesis 2:4-7 it is evident that the man lived on the earth in perfect conditions. There was no rain but there went up a mist from the earth and watered the whole face of the ground that helped every plant of the field and every herb of the field to grow. "The LORD God formed man of the dust of the ground and breathed into his nostrils the breath of life and man became a living soul".

There was a perfect rest for the man to enjoy in the presence of the LORD and have fellowship with Him. The creation of heavens and the earth and all the host of them by the God ended on the sixth day and God rested. It was God's Sabbath and not man's. It was God who rested and not man.

It is not because God was tired that He rested on the seventh day but because his creation was complete. The creation was completed in six days and on the seventh day God rested.

Notice the God created and His creation was complete and He rested. It was His act and He completed it and after that He rested because there was nothing to be created after sixth day. God rested from all His work which He had made and blessed the seventh day and sanctified it.

In the commands God gave to man He has not included that man should rest on the seventh day nor did he make it as an example for man to follow. God did not tell Adam or any of his posterity until the law was given during the period of Moses. There is not a single reference in Genesis that Noah, or Abraham, or Isaac, or Jacob or his children observed seventh day as rest day.

CHOSEN GENERATION

In Abraham was a chosen generation who came from the loins of his grandson Jacob and whom God called as "my people". (Genesis 12:7, Exodus 3:7) Abraham's son was Isaac and Isaac's son was Jacob and Jacob's sons went into Egypt as a result of famine in the land of Canaan. (Genesis 37:1)

The children of Israelites were under the bondage of slavery under Pharaoh for four hundred and thirty years. (Exodus 12:40) They cried and suffered under Pharaoh and the LORD heard their prayers. The LORD saw the affliction of His people who were in Egypt and knew their sorrows. (Exodus 3:7). Therefore, the LORD delivered them from the bondage of slavery under Pharaoh and made a covenant with them (Exodus 12:51).

After delivering the children of Israel from the slavery under Pharaoh God led them through wilderness to Canaan. While they were on their journey God gave them Ten Commandments to follow. Along with the Ten Commandments God also gave them promises such as:

"And said, If thou wilt diligently hearken to the voice of the LORD thy God, and wilt do that which is right in his sight, and wilt give ear to his commandments, and keep all his statutes, I will put none of these diseases upon thee, which I have brought upon the Egyptians: for I am the LORD that healeth thee". (Exodus 15:26)

"Now therefore, if ye will obey my voice indeed, and keep my covenant, then ye shall be a peculiar treasure unto me above all people: for all the earth is mine" (Exodus 19:5)

That was the essence of the Old Covenant. God spoke to Moses and said to him to give instructions to the children of Israel to keep the Ten Commandments and if they obeyed His voice and kept all His commandments none of the diseases that Egyptians suffered would come on them and they will be a peculiar treasure unto God above all people.

Abraham obeyed God's voice even before the Ten Commandments were given to the children of Israel and God blessed Abraham (Genesis 26:5). God did not include the Sabbath Command in the days of Abraham. This commandment was given to the children of Israel much later in the days of Moses (Exodus 20:1-17).

God said to the children of Israel through Moses that He would show mercy unto thousands of them that love Him and keep His commandments (Exodus 20:6). One such commandment, which was fourth one of the Ten Commandments, was:

"Remember the sabbath day, to keep it holy". (Exodus 20:8)

The LORD reiterated about Sabbath in Leviticus 23:1-3

"And the LORD spake unto Moses, saying, Speak unto the children of Israel, and say unto them, Concerning the feasts of the LORD, which ye shall proclaim to be holy convocations, even these are my feasts. Six days shall work be done: but the seventh day is the sabbath of rest, an holy convocation; ye shall do no work therein: it is the sabbath of the LORD in all your dwellings"

Obviously the Ten Commandments were given to the children of Israel and the fourth Command to keep Sabbath as holy was also to them. There is not one single reference which shows that the Gentiles were asked to keep the fourth commandment.

THE PUNISHMENT FOR NOT KEEPIG SABBATH

God not only gave the commandment of Sabbath to the Nation Israel but He also detailed the punishment for not keeping the Sabbath. Exodus Ch. 31:12-18 say that the LORD spoke to Moses saying to him that he should speak to the children of Israel and affirming that truly they should keep the Sabbaths that He commanded them to keep.

The LORD said that it is a sign between Him and the Nation Israel throughout their generations. The demand from God that they should keep the Sabbaths was given because they were chosen generation and they are sanctified as the people of the LORD.

They were asked to keep the Sabbath as it was holy unto them and the consequence of violation of the commandment from God was that they shall not only be cut off from among His people, but shall be put to death. God said that every one of the Nation Israel who defiles the Sabbath shall surely die. They were asked to take perfect rest on the day of Sabbath.

Six days they shall work, as commanded by God, and on the seventh day they shall do no servile work therein. God made heaven and earth and on the seventh day He rested and this pattern was to be followed by every one of the children of Israel.

It was given as a perpetual commandment along with other commandments after communing with Moses on the Mount Sinai. God wrote the Ten Commandments with his finger on the two tables of stone that became the testimony.

Later, these two tables containing The Ten Commandments were kept in the Ark of the Testimony in the most Holy of Holies of the Tabernacle as a testimony for remembrance perpetually.

DID ISRAELITES KEEP SABBATH?

"Six days shall work be done, but on the seventh day there shall be to you an holy day, a sabbath of rest to the LORD: whosoever doeth work therein shall be put to death". (Exodus 35:2)

Note the severity of the punishment God detailed for not keeping the Sabbath. God said whoever violated His commandment shall be cut off from His people and shall be put to death.

 Neither they nor their sons, or their daughters, or manservant, or their maidservants, or their ox, or their donkeys, or any of their cattle or the strangers who became proselytes by showing allegiance to them and their God were allowed to do any work on the seventh day. The demand from

The LORD that they should keep Sabbath was given to them because He brought them out from Egypt with a mighty and outstretched arm (Deuteronomy 5:12-15).

God provided the children of Israel 'manna' from heaven to eat six days a week and on the seventh day they were commanded not to go out to gather the 'manna'. They were asked to gather the heavenly bread 'manna' on the sixth day for the seventh day also and nothing more.

But some of them went out and gathered on the sixth day more than what is required for sixth day and seventh day and some went out on the seventh day to gather the food for them. He gathered more did not have extra food, nor did the one who went out to gather on the seventh day found any food. This shows that the children of Israel disobeyed God and tried to do work on seventh day. (Exodus 16:25-31)

Ye shall kindle no fire throughout your habitations upon the sabbath day. (Exodus 35:3)

A specific incident is pointed out Numbers 15:32-36 where a case of a man who violated Sabbath is mentioned. While the children of Israel were in the wilderness they found a man who violated the fourth commandment about Sabbath.

The man was gathering sticks on the day of Sabbath. It might appear to be trivial but the violation deserved punishment according to the law. They brought the man to Moses and Aaron and before the entire congregation.

Even though law was known to Moses and Aaron, they depended on God to receive a decision about the course of action to be taken and until the time God gave instruction the man was put in a ward. The LORD said to Moses that the man should be surely put to death and the entire congregation shall stone him with stones outside the camp. In obedience to the instructions received from the LORD they took him outside the camp and stoned him unto death.

The only permitted work on the Sabbath day was that which helps in eating food (Exodus 12:16). The very essence of the law was to point the guilt of a man and condemn him unto punishment he deserved for violating the law.

The Mosaic Law provided only for the covering of sin and did not provide any solution for complete removal of sin. It was only through the blood of Lord Jesus Christ shed on the cross that a man's sin can be completely removed. Salvation is by grace through faith in Lord Jesus Christ.

No amount of good works or keeping any of the provisions of Mosaic Law could earn salvation for anybody. The sacrifices and offerings detailed in the book of Leviticus could only provide temporary remedy for the sin of man.

Everyone failed to keep one commandment or the other of the Ten Commandments given by the LORD. It is, therefore, insisting on keeping any of the Ten Commandments to earn salvation or be justified before the Law is no more can be considered right.

Lord Jesus died once and for all for our sins, and was buried and rose from the dead without seeing any corruption. Sabbath was made for man and it is not vice versa. Jesus said He was the Lord of the Sabbath.
"And he said unto them, The sabbath was made for man, and not man for the Sabbath" (Mark 2:27)

"For the Son of man is Lord even of the sabbath day" (Matthew 12:8)

It is very clear in the present dispensation that it is impossible to keep Sabbath on Saturday for the simple reason that if we fail to keep Sabbath on Saturday we have to offer either sacrifice to cover our sin or get stoned unto death.

As written in Hebrews 10:26 there remains no more sacrifice for us except for the sacrifice offered once and for all by our Lord Jesus Christ by offering Himself on the cross for our sins. Surpassing our bad works with our good works is not the solution detailed in the Scripture for violating the Sabbath.

WHY DO WE KEEP SABBATH ON SUNDAY?

Sabbath is never changed from seventh day to eighth day but then when Jesus was crucified on the cross the veil in the temple was rent into two from top to bottom signifying that in Jesus the Mosaic Law is fulfilled and we are free from that Law.

It is the resurrection day, which is Sunday that we take rest on. Man surely needs rest one day at least in a seven day period and it is good that we take rest. It is on the seventh day rest could be taken and not particularly on Saturday. Apostle Paul says...

"Let no man therefore judge you in meat, or in drink, or in respect of an holyday, or of the new moon, or of the sabbath days" (Colossians 2:16).

In addition we see in Acts 20:7 the disciples came together on the first day of the week and broke bread. In 1 Corinthians 16:2 we see that on the first day of the collections were made as God prospered them.

As we read in Acts 15th Chapter certain men came down from Judea and misled brethren that unless they are circumcised there is no salvation for them, but then Paul and Barnabas took severe exception to this demand and in the Jerusalem Peter spoke about the yoke of Mosaic Law that they were willingly taking up again on themselves in spite of redemption from it was gained through the sacrifice of Lord Jesus Christ. It is, therefore, evident that the Church does not need to observe Sabbath.

CHAPTER 8
GNOSTICISM – FALSE TEACHING AND IT IS HERESY

Apostle Peter was not dealing with a minor subject of difference of opinion or misinterpretation of scriptures when he wrote that "...there shall be false teachers among you, who privily shall bring in damnable heresies, even denying the Lord that bought them, and bring upon themselves swift destruction. And many shall follow their pernicious ways; by reason of whom the way of truth shall be evil spoken of" (2 Peter 2:1-2) but he was dealing with a subject of damnable heresies.

Peter was dealing with major issue of false teachers who pervert the true teaching of Lord Jesus Christ and diminish His deity to the level of human beings or of Satan. In his days the teaching of 'Gnosticism' was prevalent and it was like a thorn in the flesh for Christians. Gnosticism is false teaching and it is heresy.

It can be seen from the Scriptures that the disciples of Jesus practiced Jewish Christianity and that is the reason why we read Peter was saying: "Repent, and be baptized every one of you in the name of Jesus Christ for the remission of sins, and ye shall receive the gift of the Holy Ghost" (Acts 2:38)

Later Pauline Christianity rejected Jewish Christianity and Peter consented to Paul's teaching in Jerusalem Council and Pauline Christianity has come to be accepted by majority of Christians.

"And when there had been much disputing, Peter rose up, and said unto them, Men and brethren, ye know how that a good while ago God made choice among us, that the Gentiles by my mouth should hear the word of the gospel, and believe. And God, which knoweth the hearts, bare them witness, giving them the Holy Ghost, even as he did unto us; And put no difference between us and them, purifying their hearts by faith. Now therefore why tempt ye God, to put a yoke upon the neck of the disciples, which neither our fathers nor we were able to bear?" (Acts 15:7-10)

However, Paul circumcised Timothy to avoid stir and commotion among Jews and followers of Paul.

"Him would Paul have to go forth with him; and took and circumcised him because of the Jews which were in those quarters: for they knew all that his father was a Greek" (Acts 16:3)

There were three major beliefs during the time when Peter wrote his 2nd epistle.

1. Jewish Christianity (with rituals like circumcision, baptism still in existence)
2. Gnosticism
3. Pauline Christianity rejecting circumcision, Mosaic Law etc., and emphasizing more on Grace.

Peter was struggling with Gnostics on one side and on the other side Jews who did not believe Jesus as their Messiah and also with Greek Mythology, Spirits etc.

Gnosticism is a belief of self-understanding, self-realization and uniting with God. Gnostics devalue matter and regard spirit as the reality. Christian Gnostics believed in spiritual knowledge and experience as the road to salvation and side stepped faith, Church and sacraments.

Gnostics believe that Demiurge an evil god created universe and men are held captive in this universe in material world and that special knowledge, which is 'gnosis' is needed to achieve purity to emulate far too pure God.

According to them material world is evil and, therefore, man needs to practice abstinence from material wealth etc. They believe that Jesus came down from Spiritual world and was their good teacher. They do not believe in atoning sacrifice of Lord Jesus Christ and say that Jesus had a sprit body and not a physical body on His resurrection.

Gnosticism promoted avoiding not only Jewish dietary restrictions and circumcision but also promoted avoiding commandments against adultery and fornication; in other words Gnosticism did not consider adultery and fornication as sins.

Gnosticism was one of the first doctrines in early days of Christianity to be rejected as heresy when Peter and Paul were preaching. Gnostics suffered not only under Christians but also under Islamic Regimes.

Gnosticism promoted avoiding not only Jewish dietary restrictions and circumcision but also promoted avoiding commandments against adultery and fornication; in other words Gnosticism did not consider adultery and fornication as sins.

Gnosticism was one of the first doctrines in early days of Christianity when Peter and Paul were preaching and this belief was the first one to be declared as heresy. Gnostics suffered not only under Christians but also under Islamic Regimes.

Scriptures have directly condemned false teaching and false teachers.

*"As I besought thee to abide still at Ephesus, when I went into Macedonia, that thou mightest charge some that they teach no other doctrine, Neither give heed to fables and endless genealogies, which minister questions, rather than godly edifying which is in faith: **so do**"* (1 Timothy 1:3-4)

"For many deceivers are entered into the world, who confess not that Jesus Christ is come in the flesh. This is a deceiver and an antichrist" (2 John 1:7)

"For there are certain men crept in unawares, who were before of old ordained to this condemnation, ungodly men, turning the grace of our God into lasciviousness, and denying the only Lord God, and our Lord Jesus Christ" (Jude 1:4)

Indented to
http://www.newworldencyclopedia.org/entry/Gnosticism

CHAPTER 9
CIRCUMCISION

"But there rose up certain of the sect of the Pharisees which believed, saying, That it was needful to circumcise them, and to command them to keep the law of Moses". (Acts 15:5)

Certain men (who were also known by some as "Judaizers") were propagating that those who desire to have salvation need to be circumcised according to Old Testament Laws. This was a false teaching put forward by "Judaizers". Paul and Barnabas took great exception to this teaching and disputed with them. They all determined that Paul, Barnabas and certain others should go to Jerusalem and sort out this dispute.

On their way they passed through Phenece and Samaria and declared conversion of the Gentiles. This caused a great joy among the brethren. When they reached Jerusalem the elders and apostles and the whole Church received them and they gave their testimonies declaring the good things God did to them and how favorable He was to them. (Ref. Acts 15:1-4)

Paul taught that circumcision is not required for salvation and it was accepted in Jerusalem Council with Peter supporting Paul's teaching, and yet Paul circumcised Timothy to avoid stir and commotion among Jews.

"Him would Paul have to go forth with him; and took and circumcised him because of the Jews which were in those quarters: for they knew all that his father was a Greek" (Acts 16:3)

While circumcision in itself is not sin and it does not prevent anyone entering into heaven, believing that circumcision is necessary for salvation is in error and such teaching can be categorized as false teaching because it undermines the efficacy of the blood shed by Lord Jesus Christ.

It also gives idea that the finished work of Lord Jesus Christ is not enough to receive salvation but something more in the form of works need to be done for salvation. Believing that circumcision is required for salvation renders a teaching that a man has to become proselyte for being saved.

Proselytes were those strangers in the land of Israel who, if they desired to join Israelites, live among them in their land, they could do so without observing ceremonial laws. No hardships were laid on strangers who wished to join them and live among them. The third generation of Egyptians and Edomies (lineage from Esau) were included as strangers who could be proselyted but this privilege was not given to Ammonites and Moabites.

However, if they wished to join Israelites and participate in the Passover festival they have to necessarily be circumcised. Passover was a privileged festival of Israelites and strangers could not participate in it unless they were circumcised.

"Ye shall not eat of anything that dieth of itself: thou shalt give it unto the stranger that is in thy gates, that he may eat it; or thou mayest sell it unto an alien: for thou art an holy people unto the LORD thy God. Thou shalt not seethe a kid in his mother's milk" (Deuteronomy 14:21)

"And he that blasphemeth the name of the LORD, he shall surely be put to death, and all the congregation shall certainly stone

him: as well the stranger, as he that is born in the land, when he blasphemeth the name of the LORD, shall be put to death" (Leviticus 24:16)

"And thou shalt rejoice before the LORD thy God, thou, and thy son, and thy daughter, and thy manservant, and thy maidservant, and the Levite that is within thy gates, and the stranger, and the fatherless, and the widow, that are among you, in the place which the LORD thy God hath chosen to place his name there" (Deuteronomy 16:11)

Proselytization in the New Testament period is condemned by Lord Jesus Christ because those who accept Him as Savior do not need to become Israelites but they become members of the Church, and He is the head of the Church and those saved, irrespective of Jew or Gentile, are the members of His Body.

Woe unto you, scribes and Pharisees, hypocrites! for ye compass sea and land to make one proselyte, and when he is made, ye make him twofold more the child of hell than yourselves. (Matthew 23:15)

While this is so, circumcising a man for any other reason, such as circumcising on medical reasons, is not a sin. Thus the issue of circumcision was nailed down in the council at Jerusalem to evolve a clear doctrine and the issue was resolved.

There is no such dispute or resolution evolved in the case of baptism as to whether or not Baptism is required for salvation, or Pre-tribulation rapture is right or Post-tribulation rapture is right. The pros and cons interpretations are man-made either from Darby or from Bullinger. One group might hold the others in errors. It is generally accepted by us that Baptism is not required for salvation, yet every believer has to testify in water baptism because it signifies one's death, burial and resurrection with Christ. Similarly the teaching of Pre-tribulation rapture has stood the test of time and it is the right teaching that needs to be followed.

CIRCUMCISION PROFITS NOTHING

"And he gave him the covenant of circumcision: and so Abraham begat Isaac, and circumcised him the eighth day; and Isaac begat Jacob; and Jacob begat the twelve patriarchs". (Acts 7:8)

Admonishing Galatians time and again, Apostle Paul continues to emphasize on the fact that there is salvation only in Jesus through faith by grace and not by law and works associated with it.

Getting entangled with law and with the thought that they need to do something to be saved, is tantamount to be under the yoke of bondage. About circumcision he condemns it and says that if anyone is of the belief that circumcision is necessary for salvation or for justification, the obsession of such thought will not profit them and Christ and his blood is of nothing to them.

Everyone, who is circumcised, becomes debtor to the whole law and Christ and his sacrifice has nothing for him. We are reckoned as righteous only by faith in Jesus and by his grace. Neither circumcision nor un-circumcision avails anything to a believer in Christ.

While giving an answer to the high priest Stephen says that Abraham circumcised Isaac on the eighth day in compliance to the covenant that existed between God and him. It continued in the Old Testament among the children of Israel.

But during the period of Acts of the Apostles when Peter was speaking the Holy Spirit was poured out on the Gentiles as well. The Jews who were circumcised were surprised to see that on the Gentiles also the gift of the Holy Spirit was poured.

"And they of the circumcision which believed were astonished, as many as came with Peter, because that on the Gentiles also was poured out the gift of the Holy Ghost". (Acts 10:45)

As we read through Acts 11th Chapter we see that Peter was accused of joining with Gentiles but then he expounded to them as to how God revealed to him that he should not treat unclean that which God has cleansed. (Acts 11:9)

In Romans Chapter 2 Paul condemns the thought that circumcision can save a person. (Romans 2:27-29)

Walking in the Spirit and hatred of lust of the flesh are necessary on the part of a believer to lead a holy life. One great truth a believer has to understand is that flesh lusts against the Spirit and the Spirit against the flesh and these are contrary to each other. If we are of the Spirit and are led by the Spirit we are not under the law and would not yield to the desires of the flesh.

After having known of the love of God through His one and only begotten son, Jesus, why would we turn yet unto beggarly elements like observing the days, months, times and years, and be subject again to be under the bondage of the law?

When the price for our sin and redemption is already paid for, why would we turn again to work for our salvation by ourselves? Salvation is available free of cost; the price is already paid for. All that is needed on the part of sinner is to believe that Jesus paid the price of his sin on the cross, and that he needs to believe in his heart this fact and accept him as his personal Savior.

Apostle Paul blesses those, who do not voluntarily subject themselves to be under the yoke of law, but accept Christ's death upon the cross. He says fulfilling the law of Christ is more important than that of the Old Testament laws. No one should boast of himself or glory himself but everyone should glorify Lord Jesus Christ, whose marks were borne by not only Apostle Paul but all those, who realize the efficacy of the blood of Lord Jesus Christ.

"For circumcision verily profiteth, if thou keep the law: but if thou be a breaker of the law, thy circumcision is made uncircumcision". (Romans 2:25)

BAPTISM

Baptism is external evidence of having been saved and it is witnessing to the world about the salvation one has received. Baptism is not mandatory for receiving salvation. It is an external evidence of having accepted Jesus Christ as personal savior and, therefore, every saved one should be baptized. Christ has finished all the works on the cross of Calvary and there is no requirement for us to have baptism as the mandatory condition for receiving salvation.

In comparison to the issue of circumcision, the issue as to whether or not it is sin to baptize a believer is not sorted out as a doctrine that should be followed meticulously.   There is more of evidence in Peter's preaching that baptism is required for salvation. Paul's teaching does not show an evidence to lay baptism as a condition for salvation. This is the reason why the issue as to whether Baptism is mandatory for salvation has become an argumentative issue.

Paul never said Baptism is mandatory for salvation but he baptized Crispus and Gauis. He said...

For Christ sent me not to baptize, but to preach the gospel: not with wisdom of words, lest the cross of Christ should be made of none effect. (1 Corinthians 1:17)

When we read the whole context from verse 10-17 Paul is seen discussing about Baptism and he asked a question...

Is Christ divided? was Paul crucified for you? or were ye baptized in the name of Paul? I thank God that I baptized none of you, but Crispus and Gaius; (1 Corinthians 1:13-14)

Let us look at what Peter and Paul have to say about Baptism.

Peter said...

Then Peter said unto them, Repent, and be baptized every one of you in the name of Jesus Christ for the remission of sins, and ye shall receive the gift of the Holy Ghost. (Acts 2:38)

The like figure whereunto even baptism doth also now save us (not the putting away of the filth of the flesh, but the answer of a good conscience toward God,) by the resurrection of Jesus Christ: (1 Peter 3:21)

Paul said:

Know ye not, that so many of us as were baptized into Jesus Christ were baptized into his death? Therefore we are buried with him by baptism into death: that like as Christ was raised up from the dead by the glory of the Father, even so we also should walk in newness of life. For if we have been planted together in the likeness of his death, we shall be also in the likeness of his resurrection: Knowing this, that our old man is crucified with him, that the body of sin might be destroyed, that henceforth we should not serve sin. For he that is dead is freed from sin. Now if we be dead with Christ, we believe that we shall also live with him: Knowing that Christ being raised from the dead dieth no more; death hath no more dominion over him. For in that he died, he died unto sin once: but in that he liveth, he liveth unto God. (Romans 6:3-10)

Great Commission says:

Go ye therefore, and teach all nations, baptizing them in the name of the Father, and of the Son, and of the Holy Ghost: (Matthew 28:19)

Baptism is not mandatory for salvation, yet baptism signifies a believer's death, burial and resurrection with Christ.

CHAPTER 10
PAUL REBUKES PETER

"But when I saw that they walked not uprightly according to the truth of the gospel, I said unto Peter before them all, If thou, being a Jew, livest after the manner of Gentiles, and not as do the Jews, why compellest thou the Gentiles to live as do the Jews?" (Galatians 2:14)

Apostle Paul rebuked Apostle Peter on a reason and that was surely a very stiff and open rebuke. It was not a private rebuke or admonition but a strong reproof of what Peter did. Did Peter deserve rebuke?

According to the prevailing situation the rebuke was appropriate. Man is saved by grace through faith in Jesus and not by works or Mosaic Law. Paul surely taught the right doctrine about salvation. But did Peter and Paul preach different gospels? No. If Peter preached different Gospel he could be called accursed.

"But though we, or an angel from heaven, preach any other gospel unto you than that which we have preached unto you, let him be accursed" (Galatians 1:8).

Did you hear any one giving more importance to Paul than to Peter? Beware of doctrines from such an one! Either he is misguiding out of innocence or deliberately diverting to another doctrine! All the disciples preached salvation by Grace through faith in Jesus.

Peter's audience was initially of Jews and he was obedient to the commission from Jesus. Peter and Paul had different assignments in the beginning, but not to cover their whole ministry. Peter was hypocritical when he sat to eat with Gentiles and then he withdrew from them on seeing when he saw James and others.

"For before that certain came from James, he did eat with the Gentiles: but when they were come, he withdrew and separated himself, fearing them which were of the circumcision".
(Galatians 2:12)

That was the reason why Paul said …

"But when Peter was come to Antioch, I withstood him to the face, because he was to be blamed". (Galatians 2:11)

Paul spoke on Peter's face so confidently and bluntly that Peter was wrong on his hypocritical behavior thus affirming that Paul was equal in status as of Peter and other disciples to be called as an Apostle of Jesus Christ.

Paul's confrontation with Peter was like a younger brother pointing a mistake of elder brother openly because of the offense elder brother had caused openly. Paul said that the Gospel of preaching to Jews was given to Peter and of Preaching to Gentiles was given to Paul.

(For he that wrought effectually in Peter to the apostleship of the circumcision, the same was mighty in me toward the Gentiles) (Galatians 2:8)

We do not have sufficient evidence in the Scriptures about the time gap between Peter's preaching to Jewish audience and to Cornelius, an uncircumcised Gentle and then to other Gentiles.

It is purely speculation that Peter did not preach to Gentiles. Peter surely knew the commission given in Acts 1:8. Peter did not retort at the rebuke of Paul; but rather he supported Paul at Jerusalem council in very gentlemanly way.

"And when there had been much disputing, Peter rose up, and said unto them, Men and brethren, ye know how that a good while ago God made choice among us, that the Gentiles by my mouth should hear the word of the gospel, and believe". (Acts 15:7)

Peter approved Paul's message, which shows that Paul is not greater than Peter to say that God gave Paul an extra-ordinary authority over Peter and on doctrines. This is a very strong point a group of believers contend saying Paul had the authority over the doctrines of salvation to Gentiles.

"And account that the longsuffering of our Lord is salvation; even as our beloved brother Paul also according to the wisdom given unto him hath written unto you" (2 Peter 3:15)

Before we go further on why Paul rebuked Peter it would be better to know What Jesus said about Peter. The word 'Church' appears in the New Testament first in Matthew 16:18 where Jesus said to Peter that He was the rock upon which Jesus would build His Church and that the gates of hell shall not prevail against it.

The Lord added to the Church daily such as should be saved (Acts 2:47). But if we closely ponder on the personal behavior and Character of Peter we see that Peter was always very quick to take some decision and then repent; he was rather impetuous, or impulsive.

Peter said he would not deny Jesus but denied Jesus and later repented. When Jesus spoke of his forthcoming death, Peter said it should not happen and Jesus said to Peter "Get thee behind me, Satan" Matthew 16:22, 23).

When Jesus was about to wash Peter's feet he resisted and Jesus said to Peter that if He did not wash Peter's feet he would not have part with Jesus. Then, Peter said to Jesus "... Lord, not my feet only, but also my hands and my head. (John 13:9). After resurrection of Jesus Peter said "I go fishing" rather than showing interest in finding where Jesus was (John 21:3) and just after a while when Peter saw Jesus his reaction is seen in John 21:7

"Therefore that disciple whom Jesus loved saith unto Peter, It is the Lord. Now when Simon Peter heard that it was the Lord, he girt his fisher's coat unto him, (for he was naked,) and did cast himself into the sea"

But then it was Apostle Peter who proclaimed the Gospel of Salvation first. The first ever preaching of Jesus Christ's death, burial and resurrection was done by Apostle Peter, who was the beloved disciple of Lord Jesus Christ. Peter stood up in the midst of the disciples, and gave few details (Acts 1:15) and then in Acts 2:24 declared that God raised Jesus from the death.

"Whom God hath raised up, having loosed the pains of death: because it was not possible that he should be holden of it" (Acts 2:24)

When Saul was encountered by Lord Jesus Christ as narrated in Acts 9 Peter was already getting ready to preach to Cornelius, an un-circumcised Gentile.

And it came to pass, that he tarried many days in Joppa with one Simon a tanner (Acts 9:43).

Thereafter, we read in Acts 10 Peter's preaching to Cornelius and about conversion of Cornelius.

Paul was chosen to bear the name of Jesus before 'GENTILES', and 'KINGS', and the 'CHILDREN OF ISRAEL.

"But the Lord said unto him, Go thy way: for he is a chosen vessel unto me, to bear my name before the Gentiles, and kings, and the children of Israel" (Acts 9:15)

Lord Jesus gave to his disciples commission that was applicable to Apostle Paul as well and that was to preach first to the Jews and then to Gentiles. Paul obeyed this commission and preached first to Jews and then to Gentiles.

"But ye shall receive power, after that the Holy Ghost is come upon you: and ye shall be witnesses unto me both in Jerusalem, and in all Judaea, and in Samaria, and unto the uttermost part of the earth". (Acts 1:8)

Paul was a Jew and a Pharisee and, therefore, he had much concern for his own people just as Jesus, who is born in Jewish family, had much concern for his own people first and then to the Gentiles.

Paul says in Philippians 3:4-8 that he was circumcised on the eighth day, of the stock of Israel, of the tribe of Benjamin, a Hebrew of the Hebrews. He had much zeal for keeping Mosaic Law and, therefore, persecuted the church before his conversion.

But after conversion he counted every gain in this world as loss for the sake of Christ. He acknowledged that Jesus was his Lord and considered every gain that had as 'dung' that he may win Christ. Paul also said in Romans 11:1 that he was an Israelite, of the seed of Abraham, of the tribe of Benjamin.

Paul's Roman citizenship by birth was an added qualification for him because many bought Roman Citizenship with a price paid for it but he was by birth a Roman Citizen. He was born in city of Tarsus, the capitol of Cilicia in Asia Minor (Ref. Nave's Topics), a city of southern Turkey, which was ruled by Roman Government (Acts 9:11, Acts 16:37, Acts 22:25-28)

"I say then, Hath God cast away his people? God forbid. For I also am an Israelite, of the seed of Abraham, of the tribe of Benjamin". (Romans 11:1)

The purpose of his laying emphasis on the fact that he was an Israelite, of the seed of Abraham, of the tribe of Benjamin was to say that in spite of his elite position in the Jewish lineage he had chosen to give out Gospel message to Gentiles.

The doctrines that he preached were never preached earlier. Even Peter's early preaching differed from what Paul taught. Paul was inspired by Jesus Christ to preach the Gospel of Grace to the world. This preaching was in contradiction to the preaching of Judaism, and, therefore, he had to suffer much persecution.

Once he was following Judaism, but then he turned against Judaism and preached Gospel of Grace. Paul preached that man is not saved by Law and works but by Grace alone. Paul said in Romans 1:16 that he was not ashamed of the Gospel of Christ because it is the power of God unto salvation to all those who believe, first to Jews and then to Gentiles. (Romans 1:16)

Apostle Paul's preaching which differed from what Judaism preached resulted in commotion, rebellion and refutations from among Jews. This was the first time Jews were listening to what Paul was saying that circumcision was not necessary to be saved; man is saved by Grace by faith in Jesus and not by works etc. Jews then rose and persecuted him.

Peter preached to Jewish audience who believed in signs that repentance was necessary for salvation followed by baptism, although he did not insist that baptism is mandatory for salvation.

"Then Peter said unto them, Repent, and be baptized every one of you in the name of Jesus Christ for the remission of sins, and ye shall receive the gift of the Holy Ghost". (Acts 2:38)

On the contrary Apostle Paul did not preach that Baptism is necessary for salvation. His main emphasis was on believing on Lord Jesus Christ and confessing with your mouth that God raised Jesus Christ from the dead. Then, there is a question.

Was Paul baptized and did he baptize? Acts 9:18 says that he was baptized. 1 Corinthians 1:13-17 show that Paul baptized and yet he says he was sent to preach the Gospel and not to baptize. Was he contradicting himself? No, what he meant was that while preaching the Gospel was his main focus baptism was secondary; that is to say baptism was not necessary for salvation.

Baptism is an external evidence of internal repentance and accepting Jesus as personal savior, who died for our sin, buried and was rose from the dead on the third day.

"That if thou shalt confess with thy mouth the Lord Jesus, and shalt believe in thine heart that God hath raised him from the dead, thou shalt be saved. For with the heart man believeth unto righteousness; and with the mouth confession is made unto salvation." (Romans 10:9-10)

Paul also preached that no man should judge another in respect of eating meat or in drink or in respect of holidays, or the new moon, or of the Sabbath days.

"Let no man therefore judge you in meat, or in drink, or in respect of an holyday, or of the new moon, or of the sabbath days" (Colossians 2:16)

Unfortunately, some Christians show Paul superior to Peter and cause divisions among Christians. Notice IF the Church did not start until transition period of early Christianity was completed at Acts Chapter 28, THEN Paul was not in the "Body of Christ" for nearly thirty years. But that was not true.

Peter and Paul had different duties to perform as per the commission. Peter, Paul and we are all one Body through Lord Jesus Christ (Galatians 3:14, Romans 12:4, 5). The "Body of Christ" which is the "Church" did not start in Apostle Paul but it started in Lord Jesus Christ.

"And he is the head of the body, the church: who is the beginning, the firstborn from the dead; that in all things he might have the preeminence" (Colossians 1:18)

CHAPTER 11
PRE-TRIBULATION RAPTURE

RAPTURE

One of the important prophesies that invites our attention, curiosity and hope is about the Second Coming of the Lord Jesus Christ. Although there is no word, namely, 'rapture' in the Bible, the meaning of this word as presented in 1 Thessalonians 4:17 is 'caught up'.

The Word of God teaches us that Lord Jesus Christ returns physically to establish His Kingdom literally on this earth for one thousand years. Jude 14th verse and 15th verse show us that Enoch prophesied that the Lord will return with ten thousand of His saints to execute judgment upon all.

'Rapture' is the first phase of the Second coming of our Lord Jesus Christ, and in this phase are included all believers in Christ. 'The dead in Christ shall rise first and the living saints shall be caught up together with them in the clouds to meet the Lord in the air'.

The blessed hope given to us is that we will be with the Lord forever. The resurrection of the dead with the glorified bodies (1 Cor.15:44) will be 'in a moment, in the twinkling of an eye at the last trump: for the trumpet shall sound, and the dead shall be raised incorruptible, and we shall be changed' (1 Cor. 15:52). This happens before the commencement of Daniel's Seventieth week that is 'great tribulation'.

In spite of the differing views about the 'rapture' one view that is consistent with the historical-grammatical interpretation of the Scriptures that survived the test of the time is the view that the living saints at the time of Lord Jesus Christ's second coming will be caught up together with the dead in Christ, who will rise to meet the Lord in the air, every man in the order as presented in 1 Corinthians 15:23 "But every man in his own order: Christ the first-fruits; afterward they that are Christ's at his coming".

For the Lord himself shall descend from heaven with a shout, with the voice of the archangel, and with the trump of God: and the dead in Christ shall rise first: Then we which are alive and remain shall be caught up together with them in the clouds, to meet the Lord in the air: and so shall we ever be with the Lord. (1 Thessalonians 4:16-17)

There are several reasons to believe that the 'rapture' precedes the 'great tribulation' and that believers in Christ will not see or be part of the 'great tribulation'. Jesus Christ's second coming will be personal and visible. The Lord will descend from heaven with a shout, with the voice of the archangel and with the 'trump of God'.

The Church (Ekklesia) is the precious possession of Lord Jesus Christ and, therefore, it is His love for the Church, and the faithfulness that He has toward His bride that He keeps His bride away from the earthly 'great tribulation', which is primarily for the earthly people and for those, who have rejected Lord Jesus Christ as their Messiah.

Those, who have accepted Jesus as their personal Savior and Lord, by confessing their sins to Him are the treasured possession of Him, and He protects them from the 'great tribulation, which is meant for the children of Israel, who have rejected Jesus as their Messiah. The two-fold purpose of Lord Jesus Christ coming to this earth is to restore the children of Israel their earthly kingdom, which God had promised to their fathers, and also for the heathen to see God's judgment on those, who sinned and rejected Him as their Savior.

The Church always remains with Him with heavenly blessings showered on them by God and are away from the earthly things. That is the reason, why when Lord Jesus Christ descends from heaven in the clouds with a shout, with the voice of archangel, those saints, who are dead in Christ shall rise first and those, who are alive and remain shall be caught up together with them in the clouds, to meet Him in the air, and thereafter we will be with Him forever.

THE SECOND COMING

The second coming of Lord Jesus is imminent. For a believer, rapture is the second coming of Jesus and for an unbeliever the second appearance of Jesus on the earth is the second coming of Jesus. The end time's prophecies are detailed for us in order that we may have faith and blessed hope of being received by Lord Jesus Christ and be with Him eternally.

The sequence of events leading to the Second coming of Jesus and his establishment of the millennial rule on the earth is disputed among Christians. However the undisputable fact is that the return of the Lord Jesus Christ and the resurrection of the dead saints from their graves followed by the living saints will be caught up is true.

The Pre-tribulation believes that the Church will not face the 'great tribulation' under Antichrist; while the Post-tribulation believes that the Church will face the 'great tribulation' under Antichrist, but will be protected by God. The doctrine of 'Rapture' of the Church for keeping it away from the 'great tribulation' in the mid-air for seven years is as disputed as the doctrine of rapture of the Church after the 'great tribulation'.

The word, 'rapture's is not found in the Scriptures; however in essence the meaning of the said word is getting caught up into the air. The rapture dealing with the believers getting caught up to meet the Lord in the clouds is undisputed among both the groups.

THE FACTS

Lord Jesus Christ's purpose of coming again to this earth is two-fold; firstly the second coming is for receiving His own to Himself and secondly, to fulfill the promises made to Israel. Church consisting of saved ones constitutes His bride and the marriage of the bride takes place according to Scriptures after the Church is caught up in the clouds, to meet the Lord in the air. To this marriage between the Lord and His bride are not invited the unsaved ones.

Lord Jesus Christ promised mansions for His Children, who believe in Him. "In my Father's house are many mansions: if it were not so, I would have told you. I go to prepare a place for you (John 14:2). Jesus promised that He was going to heaven to prepare mansions for them. This promise is given in John 14:2 and 3 and this purpose, which was a mystery in the Old Testament, is revealed in the New Testament.

The earthly blessings promised to the children of Israel will be restored unto them when Lord Jesus Christ appears on this earth, while the heavenly blessings promised to His bride are given after the Church is caught up in the clouds to meet the Lord in the air.

After seven years period of Antichrist's rule on the earth during which period unbelievers and Jews undergo God's wrath for having persecuted Jesus when He was on this earth, Jesus makes His second advent on the Mount olives, and later He rules literally for one thousand years sitting on the throne of David fulfilling the prophesies. The believers constituting His Bride will be always with the Lord.

The Church consists of all the believers in Jesus, irrespective of whether they are Jews and Gentiles The Church consisting of heavenly ones, saved in the precious blood of Lord Jesus Christ is His precious bride. The bride of Christ, which is the Church consisting of blessed ones should not be confused with the Israel. The covenants made to the children of Israel will be fulfilled on this earth. Ref: Acts 1:6, Hebrews 9:28, Romans 11:28, etc. Israel and the Church are separate and if this fact is understood clearly much dispute among Christians about the end days, about 'rapture' will fade away.

A question arises as to why believers should know about the events such as "sun be darkened, and the moon shall not give her light, and the stars shall fall from heaven, and the powers of the heavens shall be shaken", before the second coming of Jesus, if rapture takes place, before the second advent of Jesus on the earth, the answer would be that if the facts about these events are known before hand, everyone will have fear about the consequences of not believing in Jesus as one's savior.

According to Matt. 24:29 these events will take place immediately after the great tribulation days. It reads, 'Immediately after the tribulation of those days', referring to those 'great tribulation' days.

STANDING ON THE MOUNT OF OLIVES

Zechariah 14:4 "And his feet shall stand in that day upon the mount of Olives, which is before Jerusalem on the east, and the mount of Olives shall cleave in the midst thereof toward the east and toward the west, and there shall be a very great valley; and half of the mountain shall remove toward the north, and half of it toward the south".

1 Thessalonians 4:17 "Then we which are alive and remain shall be caught up together with them in the clouds, to meet the Lord in the air: and so shall we ever be with the Lord".

These prophecies tell us that Jesus will physically be on the earth to rule from Jerusalem, sitting on the throne of David. These two prophecies from Zechariah 14:4 and 1 Thessalonians 4:17 show us that Jesus will descend from heaven and after the seventieth week of Daniel's prophecy is completed He will step on Mount of Olives. He will judge nations and then rule from the throne of David for one thousand years.

Jesus is waiting until all His enemies are brought to His footstool. It is quite relevant here to meditate on the Psalm of David, where David prophesied the LORD (that is the Father) said to the Lord (that is The Son, Lord Jesus) to sit at His right hand, until He makes all His enemies his footstool.

"The LORD said unto my Lord, Sit thou at my right hand, until I make thine enemies thy footstool" (Psalms 110:1)

After the seventieth week of prophesy as mentioned in Daniel 9:24 is fulfilled Lord Jesus Christ, with his bride i.e. the Church, will step on the Mount of Olives. This is the Second Advent of Lord Jesus Christ on this earth.

The First Advent was when Jesus was born in Bethlehem in a Manger (Luke 2:7,12 and 16). Lord Jesus Christ with the resurrected saints will step on the Mount of Olives which is before Jerusalem on the east side. He returns to this earth with the armies of heaven as described in Revelation 19:14. It says:

"And the armies which were in heaven followed him upon white horses, clothed in fine linen, white and clean"

When the feet of Lord Jesus Christ touch the mount of Olives it will cleave in the midst thereof toward the east and toward the west, and there shall be a very great valley; and half of the mountain shall remove toward the north, and half of it toward the south". The people who persecuted Jesus will try to flee through this valley. This valley is called "Valley of Jehoshaphat" (Joel 3:1-2).

There was neither a valley nor is now a valley by the name of "Valley of Jehoshaphat" but this is future event. The meaning of the phrase "Valley of Jehoshaphat" is "The Lord Judges".

This is the throne of Lord Jesus from where he judges the nations of this earth. This judgment is not Great White Throne judgment, but it is the judgment of what is described as "Sheep and Goat Judgment" as we read in Matthew 25:33-46.

Until His enemies are brought to His footstool

Psalms 110:1-7 "The LORD said unto my Lord, Sit thou at my right hand, until I make thine enemies thy footstool. The LORD shall send the rod of thy strength out of Zion: rule thou in the midst of thine enemies.

Thy people shall be willing in the day of thy power, in the beauties of holiness from the womb of the morning: thou hast the dew of thy youth. The LORD hath sworn, and will not repent; Thou art a priest for ever after the order of Melchizedek.

The Lord at thy right hand shall strike through kings in the day of his wrath. He shall judge among the heathen, he shall fill the places with the dead bodies; he shall wound the heads over many countries. He shall drink of the brook in the way: therefore shall he lift up the head".

This psalm is fully a gospel concerning our Lord Jesus Christ, who executes the office of a prophet, of a priest, and of a king. The Father promises a prophetical office to Lord Jesus in verse 2, a priestly office in verse 4, and kingly office in 1, 3, and 5 to 6. The Jews never accepted this fact lest they should accept Jesus as their Messiah. Stephen gazing into heaven testifies in Acts 7:55 that he "saw the glory of God, and Jesus standing on the right hand of God". Paul an Apostle of Lord Jesus Christ wrote in Ephesians 1:20

"Which he wrought in Christ, when he raised him from the dead, and set him at his own right hand in the heavenly places"

The writer of Hebrews wrote in Hebrews 1:3 that Lord Jesus "...being the brightness of his glory, and the express image of his person, and upholding all things by the word of his power, when he had by himself purged our sins, sat down on the right hand of the Majesty on high". He is our high priest, "We have such an high priest, who is set on the right hand of the throne of the Majesty in the heavens" (Hebrews 8:1) and "...after he had offered one sacrifice for sins forever, sat down on the right hand of God" (Hebrews 10:12).

Recalling the Psalm of David, where David called Lord Jesus as his Lord and the Son of God, Jesus points this fact to Pharisees, who often tried to trap him. Pharisees of old believed that David said these verses about the Messiah, and yet the modern Pharisees denied this fact. When Jesus pointed this fact in Mark 12:36

"For David himself said by the Holy Ghost, The LORD said to my Lord, Sit thou on my right hand, till I make thine enemies thy footstool", they were speechless.

"And he said unto them in his doctrine, Beware of the scribes, which love to go in long clothing, and love salutations in the marketplaces, And the chief seats in the synagogues, and the uppermost rooms at feasts: Which devour widows' houses, and for a pretence make long prayers: these shall receive greater damnation". (Mark 12:38-40)

Immediately after the prophesy about the LORD, the Father, making all the enemies of the Son, Lord Jesus Christ, to come to his footstool is complete the second coming of Lord Jesus will take place and the Church will have rapture into the clouds to meet him in the air. The time and seasons are known only to the Father. Matthew 24:36 "But of that day and hour knoweth no man, no, not the angels of heaven, but my Father only".

The second coming of the Lord Jesus will be after the false teachers have brought in heresies and wrong doctrines among Christians and false prophets saying that Jesus has already come and he is 'here' and/or 'there' and after the revealing of the 'man of sin', the 'son of perdition', who is Antichrist. Jesus warned us to be careful not to believe when false prophets say, "Lo, here is Christ, or there..." Matthew 24:23

2 Thessalonians 2:2-3 "That ye be not soon shaken in mind, or be troubled, neither by spirit, nor by word, nor by letter as from us, as that the day of Christ is at hand. Let no man deceive you by any means: for that day shall not come, except there come a falling away first, and that man of sin be revealed, the son of perdition".

In 2 Thess.2:3 there is a reference to 'falling away'. This word 'falling away' means here that there will be apostasy. It also means that there will be deviation from the truth. It will be the beginning of sorrows after the revealing of Antichrist, when those, who hate Jesus hand over believers to persecutions. (Matt 24:9 and 10).

Yielding to such persecutions during the Great Tribulation period will come as a result of the aggressive demands from the false teachers, temptations, and worldliness. Those, who do not have enough knowledge of Jesus Christ, would yield to such persecutions, and those, who are strong enough in faith will resist such temptations, and persecutions. These persecutions are the result of 'great tribulation' from Antichrist, the 'man of sin', who is the 'son of perdition'. He will be revealed to the world, when the Holy Spirit, the restrainer ceases to work in the world to comfort the believers. Such revealing of Antichrist will not be until the Holy Spirit, the 'restrainer' is taken away from the way.

The restrainer will be taken back when the Church is raptured. The believers, who are living and waiting for the Lord Jesus Christ to come again, will be 'caught up' together with those, who are dead in Christ. The dead in Christ will rise first to meet the Lord in the air and we, who are living and remain, shall be 'caught up' together with them in the clouds to be with the Lord forever.

There is no reason for us, the believers to be sorrowful or worried about the things that shall come to pass after we are 'caught up'. It shall be the time for us, the believers to receive rewards at the 'judgment seat of Christ' which is also known as 'Bema seat'.

These rewards are given while we are with the Lord in the clouds (2Co 5:10 and 1Peter 5:4). The rewards are given for the works that the believers in Christ do on this earth.

True, we do not want to gain the whole world and lose our soul. Our works should be to gain rewards from our Lord at the 'Bema Seat', when we will be with the Lord Jesus Christ, on His coming again from heaven.

2 Thessalonians 2:13 "But we are bound to give thanks alway to God for you, brethren beloved of the Lord, because God hath from the beginning chosen you to salvation through sanctification of the Spirit and belief of the truth: It is for this blessed hope that we the believers in Christ wait for".

GOD PROTECTS HIS FOLLOWERS

When God decided to protect his precious ones whom He considered are upright and his followers he called in to a secure place before destroying the wicked who rejected Him.

Noah was just and perfect in the sight of God and he walked with God. Therefore, God commended Noah and his family to get into the Ark and be secure while he poured out his wrath against those who rejected Him.

Noah and his family were saved from the wrath of God. In similar way when God pours out His wrath against those who rejected him as their Savior he protects the Church and keep the believers away from his wrath. He saved them from destruction. He grants them eternal life to be with Him always. (Genesis 6:9, Genesis 7:16 and 1 Thessalonians 4:17). Surely the indignation shown by those who rejected Jesus as their Messiah will be paid for while those who are saved and protected are asked to be patient until He deals with them in His wrath.

"Come, my people, enter thou into thy chambers, and shut thy doors about thee: hide thyself as it were for a little moment, until the indignation be overpast. For, behold, the LORD cometh out of his place to punish the inhabitants of the earth for their iniquity: the earth also shall disclose her blood, and shall no more cover her slain". (Isaiah 26:20-21)

The comfort and security provided to the believers in Christ is seen in Zephaniah 2:3 where the prophet calls for repentance in order that they may be saved and hid during the period of Lord's anger. The prophet asks them to seek the LORD and His righteousness, and meekness in order that they may be hid in the day of the LORD's anger. Speaking to Jewish audience Jesus warned them not to be taken away by enticing words of anyone who would say that here is Christ or there! He said many will come in His name and will teach false doctrines and prophesy false. He said Antichrist, the son of perdition, will call himself as Christ. Jesus said to them to be careful and not believe him because the Son of man will come as a lightening out of the east, and shines even unto the west.

"Wherefore if they shall say unto you, Behold, he is in the desert; go not forth: behold, he is in the secret chambers; believe it not. For as the lightning cometh out of the east, and shineth even unto the west; so shall also the coming of the Son of man be. For wheresoever the carcase is, there will the eagles be gathered together". (Matthew 24:26-28)

John saw in his vision a great multitude that could not be numbered. They were from all nations and they stood before the throne of the Lamb. He saw that a great voice from heaven called those who are saved to "Come up hither" and they ascended up to heaven in a cloud while their enemies watched them.

Those who were caught up were from all nations, kindred, and people of all tongues and they stood before the throne of the Lamb, clothed in white robes, and palms in their hands. (Revelation 7:9, Revelation 11:12)

The man child in Revelation represented Lord Jesus Christ in whose blood our sins are cleansed. The loud voice said that the salvation, the kingdom of our God and the power of Christ is come. The accuser, Satan, who is also called the great dragon, that old serpent, the Devil, who deceived Eve in the Garden of

Eden, was cast out into the earth along with his fellow evil angels. Those who were overcome by the blood of the Lamb were saved and are asked to rejoice. It will be the time when Satan who will have very little time pursues and persecutes the nation of Israel during the Great Tribulation period.

"And the great dragon was cast out, that old serpent, called the Devil, and Satan, which deceiveth the whole world: he was cast out into the earth, and his angels were cast out with him. And I heard a loud voice saying in heaven, Now is come salvation, and strength, and the kingdom of our God, and the power of his Christ: for the accuser of our brethren is cast down, which accused them before our God day and night. And they overcame him by the blood of the Lamb, and by the word of their testimony; and they loved not their lives unto the death. Therefore rejoice, ye heavens, and ye that dwell in them. Woe to the inhabiters of the earth and of the sea! for the devil is come down unto you, having great wrath, because he knoweth that he hath but a short time. And when the dragon saw that he was cast unto the earth, he persecuted the woman which brought forth the man child". (Revelation 12:9-13)

Jesus himself said that he will come in the clouds of heaven with power of great glory and then all the tribes of the earth mourn and they shall see his coming. It is at that time that he shall send his angels with great sound of trumpet

and they shall 'gather together his elect from the four winds, from one end of heaven to the other'(Mathew 24:30,31). John also saw in his vision the Son of man coming in the cloud with a golden crown on his head. 'And he that sat on the cloud thrust in his sickle on the earth; and the earth was reaped'

"And I looked, and behold a white cloud, and upon the cloud one sat like unto the Son of man, having on his head a golden crown, and in his hand a sharp sickle. And another angel came out of the temple, crying with a loud voice to him that sat on the cloud, Thrust in thy sickle, and reap: for the time is come for thee to reap; for the harvest of the earth is ripe. And he that sat on the cloud thrust in his sickle on the earth; and the earth was reaped". (Revelation 14:14-16)

WE WILL BE CAUGHT UP

Second prophesy is from 1 Thessalonians 4:17, wherein it was prophesied that "Then we which are alive and remain shall be caught up together with them in the clouds, to meet the Lord in the air: and so shall we ever be with the Lord" The Scriptures reveal to us that we, the believers will be caught up in the clouds to meet the Lord in the air, and thereafter we will be with the Lord forever. Israel is still in enmity with the Lord and are still disobedient. God concluded them in unbelief.

Romans 11:28-32 "As concerning the gospel, they are enemies for your sakes: but as touching the election, they are beloved for the fathers' sakes. For the gifts and calling of God are without repentance. For as ye in times past have not believed God, yet have now obtained mercy through their unbelief: Even so have these also now not believed, that through your mercy they also may obtain mercy. For God hath concluded them all in unbelief, that he might have mercy upon all".

During the 'great tribulation' period Israel will cry for the Lord's mercy. This period is also called, "Jacob's Trouble" (Jeremiah 30:7 Alas! for that day is great, so that none is like it: it is even the time of Jacob's trouble; but he shall be saved out of it.)

Zechariah 12:10 "And I will pour upon the house of David, and upon the inhabitants of Jerusalem, the spirit of grace and of supplications: and they shall look upon me whom they have pierced, and they shall mourn for him, as one mourneth for his only son, and shall be in bitterness for him, as one that is in bitterness for his firstborn".

Lord Jesus pointed to the "...abomination of desolation, spoken of by Daniel the prophet, stand in the holy place..." (Matt 24:15). This prophesy is about the time period of the 'great tribulation' and it is seen in Daniel 9:26, and 27, and in Daniel 12:11. There it is mentioned about the abomination of desolation'. "And from the time that the daily sacrifice shall be taken away, and the abomination that maketh desolate set up, there shall be a thousand two hundred and ninety days.

JACOB'S TROUBLE

The time of Jacob's trouble, is the time of 'great tribulation' when Israel will mourn for the Lord, whom they crucified and this will make a way for the national repentance. God will have mercy on Israel and will restore to them their lost kingdom. The second coming of Jesus as seen by the left- behind Jews and unbelievers is the second appearance of Lord Jesus Christ on this earth. Then the feet of Lord Jesus' will stand upon the Mount Olives and thereafter He will rule for one thousand years literally from the throne of David.

The Lord is jealous God, and He shall not tolerate any one, who worships the idols, much less he tolerated the children of Israel. The troubles and curses they heaped upon themselves by worshipping idols, and making graven images and by doing evil things in the sight of the Lord God, provoked him to anger.

God swore saying, ".. I call heaven and earth to witness against you this day, that ye shall soon utterly perish from off the land whereunto ye go over Jordan to possess it; ye shall not prolong your days upon it, but shall utterly be destroyed. And the LORD shall scatter you among the nations, and ye shall be left few in number among the heathen, whither the LORD shall lead you." Deuteronomy 4:24-27 Even as they are scattered if they repent of their sins and call upon God as their Savior, He said He will deliver from the tribulation and gather them as one nation.

The great tribulation will be such as was never before in the whole history of mankind upon this earth, and this is the time when the children of Israel will surely confess that the Lord Jesus is their Messiah, and God will not go back on His words of restoring them their land, and every one's name will be found in the 'book'. (Dan.12:1)

Even though many Israelites have returned to their land, and also the nation of Israel was declared independent on May 15th, 1948, yet the complete gathering of the tribes from northern kingdom that were scattered after the Assyrians had taken them captive and the tribes from southern kingdom, who were taken captive by Babylonians, and thereafter by Persians is not complete.

Also, the children of Israel living in Israel are not all saved. God will use 'great tribulation', which comes under the 'the time of Jacob's trouble', for calling upon their Savior, Lord Jesus as their Messiah.

God warned beforehand that when they are in tribulation, and when all those troubles come upon them in the latter days, and if they turn to the Lord God, and be obedient to Him, He will not forget the covenant that He made with Abraham, Isaac, and Jacob and swore to them. (Ref. Deut. 4:30,31).

In Deut. 30:1-3 God said, that when the Israel realizes that He had driven them out of their country for the sins they committed, and call upon Him for mercy, obey His voice according to all that He had commanded, He will have compassion on them and gather them from all the nations, where He had scattered them.

Apostle Paul confirms in Romans 11:20 that because of their unbelief they 'were broken off', but when they repent of their sins, and realize that Lord Jesus is their Messiah, God will have compassion on them and 'All Israel shall be saved'. Ref. Rom. 11:26.

The time of this great tribulation is two-fold. Firstly, it is for heathen to realize that God will judge man for his sin, and secondly for the house of Israel to realize that Lord Jesus Christ is their Messiah forever.

God named Jacob as Israel and loved Israel more than we can imagine. He has called Israel as His first born son. To understand fully what God has done, it is necessary to go back to the beginning to see His purposes in choosing Israel. Israel's beginning occurs, not with Jacob, but with the calling of Abraham.

Genesis 12:1-3 "Now the LORD had said unto Abram, Get thee out of thy country, and from thy kindred, and from thy father's house, unto a land that I will shew thee: And I will make of thee a great nation, and I will bless thee, and make thy name great; and thou shalt be a blessing: And I will bless them that bless thee, and curse him that curseth thee: and in thee shall all families of the earth be blessed".

 It is not a name given by human but the name that is given by God; it is "Israel", which in Hebrew means God has striven, or God has saved. "And he said, Thy name shall be called no more Jacob, but Israel: for as a prince hast thou power with God and with men, and hast prevailed." Genesis 32:28

The descendants of Jacob are Israel, and to be specific, the tribe of Judah, and the tribe of Benjamin, and those, who are from the tribe of Levi are called, 'Jews' and the rest of them are called, "Israel". God has given great privilege to the "Israel" to be called as His first born. "And thou shalt say unto Pharaoh, Thus saith the LORD, Israel is my son, even my firstborn" Exodus 4:22.

COMPASSION ON GENTILES

"And, behold, a woman of Canaan came out of the same coasts, and cried unto him, saying, Have mercy on me, O Lord, thou Son of David; my daughter is grievously vexed with a devil". (Matthew 15:22)

 A woman stricken with devil approached Jesus for healing of her daughter, crying "O Lord, thou Son of David; my daughter is grievously vexed with a devil" but Jesus replied, " ... I am not sent but unto the lost sheep of the house of Israel." (Matthew 15:24)

Lord Jesus Christ's ministry on this earth was restricted to the Jews. His ministry was to establish the Kingdom of Heaven on this earth. Jesus said: "...Repent ye: for the kingdom of heaven is at hand" (Matthew 3:2)

"And saying, The time is fulfilled, and the kingdom of God is at hand: repent ye, and believe the gospel". (Mark 1:15)

Mark 7:26 says "The woman was a Greek, a Syrophenician by nation; and she besought him that he would cast forth the devil out of her daughter". Few references to show that she came from Gentile land are as follows:

"And the servant took ten camels of the camels of his master, and departed; for all the goods of his master were in his hand: and he arose, and went to Mesopotamia, unto the city of Naho". (Genesis 24:10)

"Because they met you not with bread and with water in the way, when ye came forth out of Egypt; and because they hired against thee Balaam the son of Beor of Pethor of Mesopotamia, to curse thee". (Deuteronomy 23:4)

"And finding a ship sailing over unto Phenicia, we went aboard, and set forth". (Acts 21:2)

The woman was a Gentile. Because the mission of Jesus was only towards Jews, he said to the Gentile woman...

"...I am not sent but unto the lost sheep of the house of Israel" (Matthew 15:24)

However, because of her faith in acknowledging her lowliness, when she said to Jesus, " yet the dogs eat of the crumbs which fall from their masters' table", "Then Jesus answered and said unto her, O woman, great is thy faith: be it unto thee even as thou wilt. And her daughter was made whole from that very hour".

It was indeed a dog's portion to the Gentile! Yet, there was a provision made for Gentiles. Later after his resurrection and before his ascension Jesus said to his disciples to go the Jews first and then to the people who are a mix of Jews and Gentiles, and then to the Gentiles

"But ye shall receive power, after that the Holy Ghost is come upon you: and ye shall be witnesses unto me both in Jerusalem, and in all Judaea, and in Samaria, and unto the uttermost part of the earth". (Acts 1:8)

PAUL: A MINISTR OF GOSPEL TO GENTILES.

God blessed Abraham and said, whoever blesses Abraham will be blessed and whoever curses Abraham will be cursed, and likewise, God gave the privilege to Israel only to be called as Israel. Whoever calls himself/herself a 'Jew' or 'Israel', without really being a Jew, will face the anger of the Lord. "I know thy works, and tribulation, and poverty, (but thou art rich) and I know the blasphemy of them which say they are Jews, and are not, but are the synagogue of Satan". Revelation 2:9.

It is very serious to identify oneself as "Jew" when one is not a Jew. Jacob and his descendants had all the priority in the presence of the Lord. "

The portion of Jacob is not like them: for he is the former of all things; and Israel is the rod of his inheritance: The LORD of hosts is his name". Jeremiah 10:16 yet, when it comes to the Church, the Church is His bride, heavenly possession.

The Church stands over the Israel and the Jews. The promises made to the Israel are earthly and God fulfilled most of the covenants made to them. The restoration of the kingdom unto them is yet to come. Jesus will reign from the throne of David for one thousand years after restoration of the kingdom to them. Unto this end the 'great tribulation' lasts and unto this end the delay occurs in the coming of Jesus again.

The saved ones only will be caught up into the mid-air when Lord Jesus comes for the second time. This waiting for the Lord Jesus to come to the mid-air, with the shout of Archangel, is the blessed hope of the Church, which is the bride, of the Lord. 1 Thessalonians 4:16

"For the Lord himself shall descend from heaven with a shout, with the voice of the archangel, and with the trump of God: and the dead in Christ shall rise first".

All the saved ones are the members of this "Ekklesia", which is also called the 'Church' All those, who are not saved will be on the earth when the Church gets 'caught up', which in other words is also known as rapture. "Then we which are alive and remain shall be caught up together with them in the clouds, to meet the Lord in the air: and so shall we ever be with the Lord." (1 Thess 4:17)

ANTICHRIST

Jesus warns about Antichrist in Matthew 24:4-7 and instructs his disciples to be careful about the false prophets, false teachers, and also asks that they need to pray that their flight may not be in winter. He instructs that they would hear of wars, rumors of wars, but all those things must come to pass, but still the end is not yet.

Jesus tells them in John 16:33 that he spoke unto them these things, so that they may have peace, because in this world they would have tribulation.

These tribulations are not similar to the great tribulation that the Jews and the left-behind will face during the Antichrist regime. These tribulations are the ones, which every Christian will face in his/her life, when he/she is in this world. Jesus asks all of us to be comfortable because he has overcome the world and such tribulations he faced on this earth.

The 'great tribulation' is different from the usual tribulations that we face in our lives. Great tribulation is universal, and it is not limited to a local place. It is as the world has never seen before. It would be more severe than the one that had passed by in AD 70, when many Jews were crucified upside down on the walls of Jerusalem.

Revelation 7:14 and 15 read, "...And he said to me, These are they which came out of great tribulation, and have washed their robes, and made them white in the blood of the Lamb. Therefore are they before the throne of God, and serve him day and night in his temple...". These are those, who come out of the 'great tribulation' and are before the throne of God.

The Church will be 'caught up' when Jesus comes in clouds. From among the left-behind 144,000 from the twelve tribes of Israel will be sealed during this time; 12,000 from each tribe except from the tribes of Dan and Ephraim. The tribes of Dan and Ephraim are guilty of idolatry.

Ephraim is joined to idols: let him alone. (Hosea 4:17)

The children of Ephraim, being armed, and carrying bows, turned back in the day of battle. They kept not the covenant of God, and refused to walk in his law; (Psalms 78:9-10)

Dan shall be a serpent by the way, an adder in the path, that biteth the horse heels, so that his rider shall fall backward. (Genesis 49:17)

And the LORD shall separate him unto evil out of all the tribes of Israel, (Deuteronomy 29:21)

Revelation Ch.7:4-8 give us the number that is sealed for redemption.

And I heard the number of them which were sealed:

And there were sealed an hundred and forty and four thousand of all the tribes of the children of Israel.

Of the tribe of Juda were sealed twelve thousand.

Of the tribe of Reuben were sealed twelve thousand.

Of the tribe of Gad were sealed twelve thousand.

Of the tribe of Aser were sealed twelve thousand.

Of the tribe of Nepthalim were sealed twelve thousand.

Of the tribe of Manasses were sealed twelve thousand.

Of the tribe of Simeon were sealed twelve thousand.

Of the tribe of Levi were sealed twelve thousand.

Of the tribe of Issachar were sealed twelve thousand.

Of the tribe of Zabulon were sealed twelve thousand.

Of the tribe of Joseph were sealed twelve thousand.

Of the tribe of Benjamin were sealed twelve thousand.

We will have glorified bodies just as the body of resurrected body of Lord Jesus Christ and we will be with the Lord forever and later will be in New Jerusalem that comes out of heaven. (Ref: Revelation Ch. 3:12 and Revelation Ch.21:2. But those who are saved during the Great Tribulation period will have earthly blessings rather than heavenly blessings on the New Earth.

According to the prophesy in Daniel 9:27 which reads as, "And he shall confirm the covenant with many for one week: and in the midst of the week he shall cause the sacrifice and the oblation to cease, and for the overspreading of abominations he shall make it desolate, even until the consummation, and that determined shall be poured upon the desolate", the Antichrist will promise peace for seven years but he will break in the mid-point after three and half years, and then will the great tribulation for three and half years will be upon the earth, globally, and not confined to local places.

This Antichrist will cause, "both small and great, rich and poor, free and bond, to receive a mark in their right hand, or in their foreheads: And that no man might buy or sell, save he that had the mark, or the name of the beast, or the number of his name". (Revelation 13:16-17)

John bearing witness of the Son of God, Lord Jesus Christ said in John 1st Chapter, that Jesus, who was the true Light, came into this world, and He was in the world, the world was made by Him but the world did not know him nor did His own people received Him. In Him was life but His own received Him not, and did not recognize that He was the true Messiah.

All along they waited for Him and are still waiting for a Messiah that they think would save them. How often God wanted to gather them as 'hen doth gather her brood under her wings' (Luke 13:34), but they killed prophets and stoned them that were sent to them. They received not their Messiah, and refused to come under the protective wings of God, who promised them shelter and would have accepted them and granted salvation.

 The children of Israel, who are still expecting a Messiah, would rest their false hopes on the one, who claims himself as their messiah, but he turns out to be the Antichrist.

This is the time of Antichrist, under whom the children of Israel will suffer great tribulation, such as was never before in the world, surpassing the events of AD 70, when many Jews were crucified upside down on the walls of Jerusalem, and even mothers ate their children of starvation (the events of AD 70, as recorded in the history from Josephus).

 The children of Israel will then realize that they have rested their hopes on a false Christ, and after suffering under him, will call upon the true God for mercy.

The God of Abraham, the God of Isaac, and the God of Jacob, who made covenant with them, will then receive them under His wings and give them shelter. They will realize that Lord Jesus Christ is the way, the truth and the life.

The Lord Jesus Christ will come down and stand upon the Mount of Olives as prophesied in Zechariah 14:4. The rapture of the Church takes place before the great tribulation. The fullness of the Gentiles would have come by then as written in Romans 11:25.

This was the mystery, which was hidden in the Old Testament. The grace period which is given in favor of Gentiles to have salvation over Israel would have completed by that time (2 Cor. 6:2). The Church is the bride of Lord Jesus Christ, who protects His bride from the great tribulation.

THESSALONIANS WERE MISGUIDED.

A letter was purportedly received by Thessalonians as from Apostle Paul, misguiding them that the Lord's Day had already come. Apostle Paul clears this misapprehension in the minds of Thessalonians that such a day will not come unless there be falling away first, and the 'man of sin', who is also called, the 'son of perdition' sits in the temple of God, proclaiming himself as God, and calling for worshippers to worship him.

This 'man of sin', who is also the 'son of perdition' is not yet revealed and such revealing will be done by God, at an appropriate time, which is known to Him only. This 'man of sin', is called the Wicked, whom the Lord shall consume 'with the spirit of his mouth, and shall destroy with brightness of his coming' (2 Thess. 2:1-12).

The children of Israel have not received the 'Son of God', the love of truth, and for this reason, God will make them believe that this 'man of sin' is their savior. But when they realize that the 'man of sin', who promised them peace, happiness and prosperity breaks covenant that he promised, then will the children of Israel will call upon the living God to have mercy on them.

 The 'man of sin' opposes exalting himself above all and sits in the temple at Jerusalem proclaiming himself as God. The followers of Antichrist with deceivable nature and unrighteousness would ultimately perish because they would have refused to accept the truth and opposed it in his time.

"And for this cause God shall send them strong delusion, that they should believe a lie" (2 Thessalonians 2:11)

The Church would have already been with the Lord in the mid-air by the time this 'man of sin' is revealed. Obviously Thessalonians received a false letter from someone who taught them that the day of judgment of God was near or the end of the world was near. Indeed such a day would not come until Antichrist is revealed first, and this revealing of Antichrist will not be until the Holy Spirit is taken away from this world.

Paul comforted them in a questioning tone that they will be in the presence of our Lord Jesus Christ at his coming again; and that they are the symbols of joy and glory of Paul, Silvanius and Timothy who wrote the epistle to the Thessalonians.

Apostle Paul exhorted Thessalonians to recollect about the message of salvation that he proclaimed earlier to them and how that they received the message as the truth and as the word of God rather than as the message from men. That message of God effactually worked in them and they believed.

Paul pointed to them those in the regions of Judea who always opposed and persecuted the men carrying the messages of God and how they opposed instead of honoring God. They opposed Paul when he spoke of the Gospel of God to the Gentiles and they feared that the Gentiles would be saved and would take away their portion of blessings from God.

Paul told them that wrath of God rests on them for the opposition that they caused. Indeed, Paul desired to visit them but he was hindered from some reason which he called as "Satan hindered us".

"Wherefore we would have come unto you, even I Paul, once and again; but Satan hindered us". (1 Thessalonians 2:18)

It is because the Holy Spirit is with us to convict of sin and protect us from falling into sin that we are not leaving Jesus. Every time we face a temptation God shows us alternate way to escape from sin. No sin is greater than the way that God provides to escape from it.

"There hath no temptation taken you but such as is common to man: but God is faithful, who will not suffer you to be tempted above that ye are able; but will with the temptation also make a way to escape, that ye may be able to bear it". (1 Corinthians 10:13)

Satan would easily take control of our lives if only the Holy Spirit would not help us to be firm in the Lord. But in those days when the Holy Spirit is taken away from this world evil will be rampant and it would be very easy for a person to fall into sin. That will be the time of Antichrist and he takes pleasure in misguiding people and causes abomination of desolation. Lord Jesus spoke of this abomination of desolation in Matthew 24:15

"When ye therefore shall see the abomination of desolation, spoken of by Daniel the prophet, stand in the holy place, (whoso readeth, let him understand:)".

At the end of Great Tribulation the Lord shall descend along with the Church on the mount of Olives. The Lord will consume this Antichrist with the spirit of his mouth and will destroy with the brightness of his coming.(1 Thessalonians 2:13-20 and 2 Thessalonians 2:1-12). We, the believers in Christ will be with the Lord for ever and ever.

Finally we may comfort one another with Apostle Paul's words:

"Now our Lord Jesus Christ himself, and God, even our Father, which hath loved us, and hath given us everlasting consolation and good hope through grace, Comfort your hearts, and stablish you in every good word and work". (2 Thessalonians 2:16-17)

THE FIVE JUDGMENTS

The following five judgments are seen in the Scriptures:

 (1) The Judgment at the cross (John 5:24)

 (2) The Judgment in the mid-air for distribution of rewards for saints: (Also called as 'Bema seat of Christ'. (2 Cor. 5:10)

 (3) The judgment of Jews and left-behind (Great Tribulation-Matt 24:20-21

 (4)The judgment of nations (also known as 'The Sheep and Goat Judgment)

 (5) The Judgment of the Wicked

(1) THE JUDGMENT AT THE CROSS

Verily, verily, I say unto you, He that heareth my word, and believeth on him that sent me, hath everlasting life, and shall not come into condemnation; but is passed from death unto life. (John 5:24)

It all started with Adam and Eve committing sin in the Garden of Eden, when they both ate the forbidden fruit and bringing sin not only on them, but also on the entire humanity. After the creation is ended 'God planted a garden eastward in Eden; and there he put the man whom he had formed'. (Genesis 2:8)

The first desire from God was that Adam should dress Garden of Eden and keep it, and then God commanded him that he is permitted to eat freely from every fruit, but he shall not eat of the tree of the knowledge of good and evil. ⧄The punishment God detailed for violating his command was that in the day that he eats from the tree of the knowledge of good and evil, he shall surely die. God said that it is not good that the man should be alone; therefore he decided to give him a help met for him.

God caused a deep sleep to fall upon Adam, and while he was asleep God took one of the ribs and closed up the flesh. This is the first sleep that God caused upon man in his divine power. That sleep was different from the sleep man would have every night.⧄

It was the deep sleep that God caused upon man.⧄ When Adam rose from that deep sleep he saw that the Lord gave him a woman as help mate. God had made Woman from the rib that He took it out of the man. When the woman was brought to the Adam, he called her Woman. They were both naked.

As they lived happily the serpent tricked Woman to yield to the temptation on false hopes, and the Woman saw that 'the tree was good for food and pleasant to the eyes'. The Woman took the fruit from the tree and not only she ate it, but she also gave it to her husband and he ate it too. They saw that they were naked and 'they sewed fig leaves together, and made themselves aprons'.

Later on God questioned them and punished them when each of them tried to blame the other. God made coats of skins and clothed Adam and his wife and sent them away from the Garden of Eden. ⏣@ Adam called his wife, Eve, because she was the mother of all living.

The sin that these two brought into the world was not such an easy one to be wiped out unless Jesus the Son of God came into this world and took upon Himself the sin of the world, that whosoever believes in him shall be saved. ⏣

The curse of 'death' that Adam had reaped upon himself and the whole humanity can be overcome only with the belief in Jesus as one's personal savior. Jesus said that whoever hears his word, and believes on him that sent him, has everlasting life and will not come into condemnation but will pass from death unto life. This is the first judgment when the sin is judged upon the cross and redemption is made available for man.

(2)THE JUDGMENT IN THE MID-AIR
FOR DISTRIBUTION OF REWARDS FOR SAINS:

(Also called as Bema seat of Christ)

For we must all appear before the judgment seat of Christ; that everyone may receive the things done in his body, according to that he hath done, whether it be good or bad. (2 Corinthians 5:10)

Every believer has to account for the deeds he has done on this earth in order to receive the rewards at the 'Bema seat of

Christ' He shall stand at the judgment seat of Christ also known as 'Bema Seat of Christ' not as an unbeliever to receive judgment for punishment, but for rewards he is entitled for working for the Lord.⍰ During the period of time when the believer is with the Lord and after the rapture, the Lord will honor his servants for the service they rendered unto Him when they were on this earth.⍰

 We are not to judge our brothers because we shall all stand before the judgment seat of Christ (Rom.14:10). The time will come when the Lord comes and He brings to the light every hidden things of darkness, and will show the counsels that have taken place in the hearts. While God does this in the presence of every believer at the judgment seat of Christ every man will praise God (1 Cor.4:5)⍰

Lord Jesus Christ is our life and He will appear in the clouds in glory to receive His own unto Himself and honor them with rewards.⍰ It is not the Great white Throne judgment, when those, who have not believed in Him, will be judged for their everlasting destiny in the lake of fire along with the Satan and his angels, but the judgment seat of Christ is the raised seat where He sits as the King of kings to administer justice.

There shall be no condemnation for the believers, who are in Christ, and who have not walked after the flesh, but sought to walk after the Spirit. (Rom 8:1).

God was in Christ and reconciled us unto Himself, and made us, who have trusted in Him, and confessed our sins to Him, as his heirs and did not impute our trespasses unto us, but washed our sins in the precious blood of Jesus. We are His workmanship, created in Christ unto good works and we stand worthy of our calling and deserve our rewards at the 'Bema Seat of Christ'. It is a blessed hope for believer that he will be honored for putting on Christ and for living holy life. It is at this time, when we, the believers are with the Lord, that we will be rewarded before He reveals Himself on this earth again.

(3)THE JUDGMENT OF LEFT-BEHIND (Great Tribulation- Matt 24:20-21)

Caught in their disbelief Jews have always been waiting for Messiah to come from an earthly King's family. This disbelief in the Messiah, who was their real King, has led them to reject Lord Jesus Christ, the Messiah, as their Savior.

Just as a hen gathers her chicken under her wings, God yearned to gather the children of Israel, the blessed generation through, Jesus, who was born in their clan, of the Virgin Mary from the lineage of King David, but they not only rejected Him, but also killed prophets and stoned them, who were sent to them.

Israelites rejected the true Messiah, Lord Jesus Christ. They did not accept Jesus as their Messiah even when He answered a Gentile woman saying that He was sent unto the lost sheep of Israel.

But, when the woman, who was a gentile prayed to the Lord that her daughter be healed by Him. She cried saying "O Lord, thou Son of David; my daughter is grievously vexed with a devil." (Matt 15:22), She had faith in Him and said "Truth, Lord: yet the dogs eat of the crumbs which fall from their masters' table". (Matt 15:27),

Jesus had compassion on her and granted answer to her prayer. A gentile received because Jews rejected Him. Apostle Paul writes about this mystery that is revealed in the New Testament about God accepting Gentiles in to the Church. (Ephesians 3:3-9).

The Church consisting of individual members, who have accepted Jesus as their Savior, are therefore, given the privilege over the Jews, and they are 'caught up' when the Lord himself 'shall descend from heaven with a shout, with the voice of the archangel, and with the trump of God: and the dead in Christ shall rise first: Then we which are alive and remain shall be caught up together with them in the clouds, to meet the Lord in the air: and so shall we ever be with the Lord'. (1 Thessalonians 4:16-17).

The unbelieving Jews and all others, who have not accepted Jesus Christ as their personal Savior will enter into the 70th week of Daniel, as prophesied in Daniel 9:26,27.

Those, who are saved, will be with the Lord, when all others, who are not saved that includes the Jews will left- behind to be under the reign of Antichrist. While the believers are happy with the Lord, and receive their rewards for their good works done on the earth, the unbelievers will be under the reign of Antichrist, who promises them earthly peace, pomp, honor, and wealth. In the middle of the last week (70th week), that is after completion of 3.5 years, their king, the Antichrist, will break the covenant that he made with them, and then will start the 'great tribulation'.

It is at this time that the Jews as prophesied will call upon God to have mercy on them, and God will come their rescue, and every one of them will be saved. Immediately after the tribulation of those days 'great tribulation' are over, 'the sun shall be darkened, and the moon shall not give her light, and the stars shall fall away from heaven and the powers of the heavens shall be shaken'. (Matthew 24:29).

(4) THE JUDGMENT OF NATIONS

(also known as 'The Sheep and Goat Judgment)

 The judgment of nations is distinct from the 'Great White Throne Judgment. The nations are the living ones that survive through the 'great tribulation' period, when the gentiles, who are left-behind, are judged.

This is a period after the Church consisting of believers are 'caught up' to be with the Lord for ever and ever. In Matthew 5:31-46 there is a description of the judgment that takes place after Lord Jesus Christ reveals himself at His second coming to everyone upon this earth.

These are the ones, who missed the blessings of being 'caught up' to be with the Lord Jesus for ever and ever, when He comes with the trump of God.

When the believers are 'caught up' to be with the Lord, the dead shall be raised incorruptible and shall be changed in a moment in the twinkling of an eye. Then those, who have put on Christ, shall be 'caught up' together with them in the clouds to meet the Lord in the air and they will all be with the Lord for ever and ever.

Those, who did not believe in Jesus and did not accept Him as their personal Savior miss these blessings of being 'caught up' and remain on this earth.

The dead in sins will remain in their graves and the living will see with their eyes the Lord Jesus revealing Himself upon this earth. The 'Son of man' will come with all the holy angels with him and shall sit upon the throne of glory. This was a prophecy proclaimed in Zechariah 14th Chapter.

"And his feet shall stand in that day upon the mount of Olives, which is before Jerusalem on the east, and the mount of Olives shall cleave in the midst thereof toward the east and toward the west, and there shall be a very great valley; and half of the mountain shall remove toward the north, and half of it toward the south". (Zechariah 14:4)

All nations (gentiles) will be gathered unto the Lord Jesus, when He sits on the throne of glory and He will separate one from the other just a shepherd divides his sheep from the goats. The 'sheep' refers to the saved ones, who had their salvation during the period, when the Lord with His chaste bride is in the air, and likewise the 'goats' refers to the unsaved ones.

The King, who is our Lord and Savior Jesus Christ, will then say unto those, who are on His right hand, 'Come, ye blessed of my Father' and then, the King, who is our Lord and Savior Jesus Christ, will say then say unto those, who are on his left hand, 'Depart from me, ye cursed, into everlasting fire, prepared for devils and his angels'. This judgment is also known as 'sheep and goat' judgment, when the nations (gentiles) are judged.

The words of the King at this judgment are very sharp and shrewd. To those, who are on His right hand, the King will say that when He was hungry they gave Him meat, and He was hungry they gave Him drink, and when he was a stranger, they took Him; Naked, and they clothed Him, and when He was sick they visited Him, when He was in prison, they went to see Him. The righteous on the right side of the King will be filled with the surprise and ask the King, when He was hungry, thirsty, naked, sick and in prison.

"And the King shall answer and say unto them, Verily I say unto you, Inasmuch as ye have done it unto one of the least of these my brethren, ye have done it unto me". (Matthew 25:40).

Similarly, the King, who is our Lord and Savior Jesus Christ will say very sharp and shrewd words to those, who are on His left side, that they did not give Him food when He was hungry, that they did not give him water when He was thirsty, that they did not take Him in when He was stranger, that they did not clothe him when He was naked, that they did not visit Him when He was sick, that they did not minister unto Him when He was in prison.

Those, whom the Word of God, calls as 'goats', (unsaved) ones, ask Him surprisingly, when they did not gave Him drink, food, and when was He naked that they did not clothe Him, and when was He stranger that they did not take Him in, and when He was sick that they did not minister unto Him, and when was in prison, that they did not minister unto Him.

"Then shall he answer them, saying, Verily I say unto you, Inasmuch as ye did it not to one of the least of these, ye did it not to me" (Matthew 25:45)

The blessings that the King shall give unto the righteous are that they will 'inherit the kingdom prepared for you from the foundation of the world' and the punishment the King renders unto those, who are not saved will be 'Depart from me, ye cursed, into everlasting fire, prepared for the devil and his angels'.

5. THE JUDGMENT OF THE WICKED

And I saw a great white throne, and him that sat on it, from whose face the earth and the heaven fled away; and there was found no place for them. And I saw the dead, small and great, stand before God; and the books were opened: and another book was opened, which is the book of life: and the dead were judged out of those things which were written in the books, according to their works. (Revelation 20:11 -12)

This is the 'Great White Throne judgment', which is the final judgment, where everyone, whose name is not found in the book of life is judged and 'death and hell will be cast into the lake of fire. This is the second death'. (Rev. 20:14)

POST-TRIBULATION RAPTURE

Post-tribulation believers say that Revelation refers to tribulation saints and this book places the rapture events and the saints of God on earth during the period when God's wrath is executed. They dispute that even if a single saint is on the earth during that period of time, the entire logic of pre-tribulation rapture is nullified. But, contrary to their belief these saints during the 'great tribulation' period were unbelievers until they were all given opportunity to be saved once before the second coming of Jesus, and, therefore, they missed to be the part of the Church, which is the bride of the Lamb of God, Jesus Christ.

The presence of saints during the 'great tribulation period, because they are saved during that period does not render the pre-tribulation rapture belief untenable. The persecutions that Christians suffer in this world are permitted by God; however, Paul re-assured the Thessalonians that God will destroy the persecutors. (Luke 21:12-19, John 16:1-4, 33, 2 Tim. 3:12).

Revelation 9:4, Revelation 16:2, Revelation 16:10 show to us that the wrath of God will be unleashed during tribulation on Antichrist's followers.

In 2nd Thess. 2nd Chapter Apostle Paul clarifies more about it by pointing about the apostasy that comes before that. He was trying to correct their misunderstanding. He was not saying that Antichrist will come after rapture.

The judgment of nations and white throne judgment are two different ones and they are executed under the administration of God in accordance with His plan and will. There is no judgment for believers at the 'white throne judgment' but the believers are judged for their good works at the Bema Seat of Christ in the mid-air, when they are with the Lord Jesus in the clouds after their rapture.

The Church does not witness nor see any signs when Lord Jesus Christ comes for the second time, but they are 'caught up' into the clouds to be with Him for ever and ever.

John Chapters 14 to 17 provide enough assurance and blessed hope for the believers that they will be with the Lord, and will not be partakers of 'great tribulation'. On the contrary, the signs are given for the Israel, who will see Lord Jesus coming to the earth as their Messiah, who will step his foot on the mount of Olives, as prophesied in Zechariah 14:4.

The first heaven and first earth will pass away and new heaven and new earth will come down (Rev. 21 Chapter). This is the permanent abode of the believers.

Revelation 21:27 And there shall in no wise enter into it anything that defileth, neither whatsoever worketh abomination, or maketh a lie: but they which are written in the Lamb's book of life.

 Post-tribulation-believers lack faith in themselves and are confused about the blessed glorious future with the Lord, who promised eternal life. The fear of Antichrist being revealed and their own sufferings under him, the 'man of sin', the 'son of perdition', looms large in their faces and conscience even though the Lord promised eternal joy, peace of mind, and happiness.

Lord Jesus Christ and his disciples always taught that the repent Kingdom of God is at hand. Some

Thessalonians were afraid that their own missed the resurrection. Apostle Paul correcting their misunderstanding comforts them in 1 Thessalonians. 4:13-18 that they need not fear about such things, inasmuch as the Lord Jesus Christ will himself 'descend from heaven with shout, with a voice of Archangel, with the trump of God; and the dead in Christ shall rise first:

Then we which are alive and remain shall be caught up together with them in the clouds, to meet the Lord in the air: and so shall we ever be with the Lord. Wherefore comfort one another with these words'.

Apostle Paul writes in 2 Thessalonians 3:17 that these epistles are written by himself. Thessalonians received letter as from Paul, which confused their minds that the day of Christ was already at hand, giving them a sense that they have already missed the resurrection.

Apostle Paul confirms to them that the day of Christ will not come until there come a falling away first and, therefore, none need to be deceived by such suspicious letter. He goes on to imbibe confidence in them that the lawlessness is already at work, but the 'man of sin' is not yet revealed. He writes that the Lord will consume that Wicked one with the spirit of His mouth.

The Lord will also consume even the one, who comes working the deeds of Satan showing wonders. Post-tribulation-believers miss these points and wait anxiously for the 'man of sin', that Wicked one to be revealed. For this cause, the Lord shall hand them over to their own disbelief.

Apostle Paul gives great hope that we as believers give always thanks unto God 'because God hath from the beginning chosen you to salvation through sanctification of the Spirit and belief of the truth'. (2 Thessalonians 2:13). The exhortation from Paul is that we are called unto Gospel, to receive the glory of the Lord Jesus Christ, and, therefore, we need to stand steadfast comforting one another, 'Lord Jesus Christ himself, and God, even our Father, which hath loved us, and hath given us everlasting consolation and good hope through grace'. (2 Thessalonians 2:16)

Bible speaks unto those, who surrender to the Spirit of God, the truth that is hidden from the knowledgeable and wise of this world, the fact of the Gospel of Christ, salvation and protection of His children. His own rejected Him, and that is the reason why God blinded their eyes from the truth, until the fullness of the Gentiles be come in. (Romans 11:14).

Human wisdom is helpful to know the truth and be misguided from human logic that leads them into follies and be far away from the mysteries and the truth of the living God, who reveals Himself only to those, who surrender to Him. Great men have known Jesus and read the Scriptures without profiting from them, but the foolish of this world that were chosen by God, have known Him fully and were happy in Him.

Bible speaks of Gospel, which is the good news of the Lord Jesus Christ's bearing sin of mankind, His resurrection and ascension, in different forms and perspectives.

The four different forms are:•The Gospel of the 'Kingdom of God' that deals with the fulfillment of Davidic covenant that the 'kingdom shall be established for ever before thee: thy throne shall be established for ever'. (2 Samuel 7:16).

This Kingdom of God includes the thousand year literal reign of Lord Jesus Christ from the throne of David in Jerusalem, as detailed in Zechariah 14:9 "And the LORD shall be king over all the earth: in that day shall there be one LORD, and his name one".

•The 'Gospel of Christ' that deals with the Salvation of mankind that Apostle Paul spoke of, as the 'Grace of God', that Jesus died for our sins, and that He was raised from the dead. Jesus died and was raised for our justification and we are justified because of our belief in Him.

"For we stretch not ourselves beyond our measure, as though we reached not unto you: for we are come as far as to you also in preaching the gospel of Christ" (2 Corinthians 10:14)

•The 'Gospel' that is called 'everlasting gospel', preached unto those, who did not believe in him, and who will pass through the 'great tribulation' until the last days before the last judgment. "And I said unto him, Sir, thou knowest. And he said to me, These are they which came out of great tribulation, and have washed their robes, and made them white in the blood of the Lamb". (Revelation 7:14)

•The Gospel that is called 'another gospel', which is the perversion of the Gospel of Christ. Christians are warned to be careful about this 'another gospel' by the agents of Satan, who transforms himself as the angel of light.

Apostle Paul writes about this gospel. "I marvel that ye are so soon removed from him that called you into the grace of Christ unto another gospel: Which is not another; but there be some that trouble you, and would pervert the gospel of Christ". (Galatians 1:6-7). False apostles calling themselves as apostles of Christ preach this gospel perverting the truth of the real gospel of Jesus that Apostle Paul calls as 'my gospel' in Romans 2:16, the gospel of Christ.

However, "my gospel" is not to be understood as Paul's personal Gospel, but it is the same Gospel which Peter and others preached; that is of Lord Jesus Christ's death, burial and resurrection. Paul was contradicting those who were Judaizers, who insisted on circumcision for Gentiles to be saved.

THE MILLENNIUM

God promised the children of Israel in Ezekiel 36:24 that He will take them from among the heathen, gather all of them of their countries and bring them to their own land. As a shepherd seeks out his flock when the sheep are scattered, so will the Lord seek out his sheep and deliver them from out of all places, irrespective of the conditions under which they were scattered even if that were the cloudy and dark day.

The Lord promised that He will bring them to their own land, promised unto them, in Genesis 12:1-3, Deut. 30:3, and Isaiah 43:6, and feed them upon the mountain of Israel by the rivers in the midst of all the inhabited country.

 What seems to be impossible humanly is shown as possible in Ezekiel 37:3 where it reads, "And he said unto me, Son of man, can these bones live? And I answered, O Lord GOD, thou knowest". Christian belief rests in faith in eternal God, who has shown time and again, that nothing is impossible with Him. If dry bones can resurrect, then the Word of God, which says, his children will be caught up to the clouds where the Jesus comes in clouds should not be doubted.

The vision Ezekiel saw in 37th Chapter verses 1to 14 gives a clear picture as to how God will unite the children of Israel, once divided into two nations, the northern kingdom, also known as Ephraim and Southern kingdom known as Benjamin and Judah. After the death of king Solomon, the northern kingdom was ruled by Jeroboam and the southern kingdom was ruled by Rehoboam. These two kingdoms were at war with each other.

The northern kingdom, although they were descendants of Jacob, were known as Israel, while the southern kingdom was known as Jews. The Jews and Israel were at war with each other always. Assyrians captured the northern kingdom and took them captive, while Babylonians captured the southern kingdom and took them captive.

After Persians took captive and carried away, the southern kingdom under Babylonians they could never return to the southern part of Israel. The ten tribes from the northern kingdom and the two tribes from the southern kingdom were all dispersed and scattered. The tribe of Levi, who were loyal to King David, got assimilated into both the northern kingdom and the southern kingdom.

In the prophesy detailed in Ezekiel 37th Chapter 1 to 14 God shows to us that He will unite these two kingdoms and there shall be one Kingdom. The spirit of the Lord was upon the prophet Ezekiel, and he was set in the midst of the valley that was full of bones. When the spirit of the Lord asked the prophet if the dead bones could live again, the prophet replied saying, :"O Lord God, thou knowest".

The spirit of the Lord asked the prophet to prophesy and call them as 'O ye dry bones, hear the word of the Lord'. The prophet continues as instructed by the spirit of the Lord and says that the Lord will cause breath to enter into them, and they shall live.

The prophet saw that while the bones are gathered together, the sinews and flesh came upon them and skin covered them above but there was no breath in them. Then the spirit of the Lord said to the prophet to say to the wind that the Lord God orders the to come from the four winds, and calls upon the breath, to breathe upon those slain that they may live again. The prophesy is in so strong words, that as he commanded there was a noise, and the bones came together joining bone to bone together, and sinews and flesh came upon them followed by skin covering the bones and sinews that they lived again. Those that lived again were huge in number and were an exceeding army.

The prophesy in Ezekiel 37 1-14 details as to how God resurrects the dead bones of Israel, and bring all of them together, irrespective of their former alliance to northern or southern kingdom. The dead bones come out of the graves live with sinews and flesh put on them after every bone joins to the other and skin covering them and breathe entering them, and all of them come together as a nation. The nation of Israel under Lord Jesus Christ as their messiah and literal ruler for thousand years in the future is coming. He is the Lord and He is the King of kings.

 Ezekiel prophesied saying that the word of the Lord came to him to prophesy about the unification of the divided kingdom of Israel. The kingdom that was divided into two and got scattered all over the world, will be united.

The word of the Lord asked him to take two sticks, one for Judah (the southern kingdom under Benjamin and Judah, with two tribes) and another for the northern kingdom (of Ephraim with 10 Tribes of Israel), and join one stick to the other and they will become in his hand.

When the children of Israel ask him to show what that meant, he should, as the word of the Lord said to him, that God will unite the lost ten tribes of Ephraim and the two tribes of the tribe of Benjamin and Judah into one; they shall not be two kingdoms any more, but one. They shall not defile themselves with idols, instead God says He will cleanse them. They shall be His people and He shall be their God.

Referring to David, the shepherd, the word of God points to the Lord Jesus Christ, who proclaimed that He is the Good Shepherd, will be the King over the children of Israel.

The covenant of peace that God makes with them will be an everlasting covenant with them. God promises that He will multiply them and set His sanctuary in their midst for evermore. God says the heathen will know the He is the Lord, who sanctify Israel, and in their midst will be the sanctuary for evermore. Ref. Ezekiel 37:15-28

CHAPTER 12
ARE WE LITTLE GODS

There is a false teaching that we, human beings, are little gods. This chapter counters such claim.

"Jesus answered them, Is it not written in your law, I said, Ye are gods? If he called them gods, unto whom the word of God came, and the scripture cannot be broken; Say ye of him, whom the Father hath sanctified, and sent into the world, Thou blasphemest; because I said, I am the Son of God?" (John 10:34-36)

John Chapter 10 shows us great deal of truth concerning Lord Jesus Christ, the Son of God: "Who, being in the form of God, thought it not robbery to be equal with God: But made himself of no reputation, and took upon him the form of a servant, and was made in the likeness of men" (Philippians 2:6-7)

In John Chapter 9 and 10 there is narration of a sequence of events that eventually show that Jesus is the Son of God, and He is the Very God Himself.

Jesus said:

1. He is the Good shepherd
2. Sheep hear his voice
3. Good shepherd knows His sheep
4. His sheep know that He is the Good Shepherd
5. Good shepherd protects His sheep
6. His Father gave Him the sheep and no man can pluck them out of His Father's hand
7. Jesus and the Father are ONE

The Jews then took up stones to stone him. This is the context where Jesus quoted Psalm 82 to shake the foundation of the knowledge of Pharisees and Rabbis.

In John Chapter 9 there is narration of how a blind man was healed by Lord Jesus Christ and the blind man believed Him as the Son of God and worshipped him. Pharisees, who always tried to trap Jesus on some point argued with Him many times.

When they questioned Jesus about their own condition as to whether they were blind, Jesus said to them, that He came to give sight to the blind that they may see and also make blind some like those Pharisees who see yet do not understand. Jesus said if they were blind there would not have been sin upon them but their sin remains on them because they claim that they see; but Jesus knew that they did not perceive Him or His works.

The reason why Jews took up stones to stone Jesus was that Jesus claimed to be God. Jesus said He and the Father are one. Jesus claimed that He came from the Father and He did the works of the Father. The Jews thought that Jesus was blaspheming God. Although God manifested Himself as Triune God "Jehovah" is one. The Father, The Son, and the Holy Spirit are three in one and are co-equal, co-existent but have different function to perform, yet all the Three Are One.

Deuteronomy 6:4 from the Old Testament says:

"Hear, O Israel: The LORD our God is one LORD"

Pharisees, who were good in studying the scriptures and arguing by the meaning of each phrase and word, knew this verse very well and when Jesus claimed that He and the Father are one, they had conviction in their minds that Jesus was blaspheming God.

In John 10:17 Jesus brings out excellent truth that the Father loves Him, because He lays down His life that He might take it again.

It pleased the Father to bruise the Son, put him to grief when He shall make His soul an offering for sin. Jesus died for our sake; He was buried; yet Jesus was raised from the dead on the third day as it is written. (Isaiah 53:10)

 "For he hath made him to be sin for us, who knew no sin; that we might be made the righteousness of God in him". (2 Corinthians 5:21)

"No man taketh it from me, but I lay it down of myself. I have power to lay it down, and I have power to take it again. This commandment have I received of my Father" John 10:18

As Jesus was speaking about the Father and Himself that they are one, there was a division among Jews and one section of the Jews said that Jesus had devil in him while others argued that if he had devil in him, how would he heal the blind?

Jesus was walking in the temple in Solomon's porch on a feast day. It was the Feast of Dedication in winter when Jews surrounded him and asked him to say plainly if Jesus was the Christ. Jesus answered them and said that He told them already, yet they did not believe Him or His words or works that He did in His Father's name.

Jesus said that the works of the Father that He did bear witness that He was the Son of God and He and the Father are one. His sheep hear His voice and they follow him, but they did not believe him or His works because they are not His sheep as He said before. That was the time when Jews took up stones to stone him to death, because they thought Jesus was blaspheming and blaspheme is punishable by stoning to death.

"Bring forth him that hath cursed without the camp; and let all that heard him lay their hands upon his head, and let all the congregation stone him. And thou shalt speak unto the children of Israel, saying, Whosoever curseth his God shall bear his sin. And he that blasphemeth the name of the LORD, he shall surely be put to death, and all the congregation shall certainly stone him: as well the stranger, as he that is born in the land, when he blasphemeth the name of the LORD, shall be put to death". (Leviticus 24:14-16)

"And thou shalt stone him with stones, that he die; because he hath sought to thrust thee away from the LORD thy God, which brought thee out of the land of Egypt, from the house of bondage" (Deuteronomy 13:10). Compare also Deuteronomy 17:3-5, and 2 Samuel 12:14

This was not the first time Jews took up stones against Jesus to stone Him to death. John 8:51-59 show us that Jesus said that whoever keeps His words will not see death. Jesus was obviously affirming that those who believe in Him and keep His words will have eternal life, but Jews misunderstood him and said Abraham and prophets died and how that Jesus was saying that whoever keeps His words will not taste death.

Jesus said that their father Abraham rejoiced to see His day and saw it, and was glad (John 8:56). Jews, indeed, thought Jesus was speaking blasphemy because he was not yet fifty years old but he said before Abraham He was there. Jews took up stones to stone Him to death, but Jesus being divine walked away from their midst unharmed.

In John Chapter 10 also we see that they tried to stone Jesus in vain, and Jesus walked away from their midst unharmed. Jesus laid down His life when it was due time for Him to lay down His life. He laid down His life when it was appointed time for Him to lay down His life and took it back when it was due time. The Body of Jesus did not see any corruption but was raised from the dead on the third day and He appeared to His disciples and many others who belonged to Him for forty days and then ascended into heaven. He is seated on the right hand of the Majesty and will come soon.

Jews said to Jesus that for they were not there to stone him for the good works He had been doing but for alleged blaspheme. That was the time when Jesus questioned them and shook their foundation of presuppositions. They thought Jesus was an ordinary man and that he was blaspheming God. They are aware of the books of Moses and more clearly Deuteronomy 6:4 according to which they, who were the children of Israel, were not supposed to have any other gods before Him. They knew that Jehovah is the true God and there is only one God, who is their LORD.

"Hear, O Israel: The LORD our God is one LORD" Deuteronomy 6:4

In Exodus Chapter 20 the Ten Commandments were given and the LORD said:

"I am the LORD thy God, which have brought thee out of the land of Egypt, out of the house of bondage. Thou shalt have no other gods before me. Thou shalt not make unto thee any graven image, or any likeness of anything that is in heaven above, or that is in the earth beneath, or that is in the water under the earth" (Exodus 20:2-4)

That was a commandment that before the true God of Israel there shall be no other gods and they shall not worship any other god other that the LORD their God, who brought them out the land of Egypt redeeming them the bondage of slavery. But here in this context Jesus was saying that He was the Son of God, and He and the Father are one. Yet, his quotation from Psalm 82:6 was not to prove his coming to this world as "Messiah", or that Psalm 82:6 was a prophecy about Him.

The reason why Jesus quoted few verses from Psalm 82 was to thrash them on their own argument, and to shake the foundation of their presuppositions. Jesus did thrash their argument successfully and they walked away from them unharmed. To understand what Jesus was saying it is necessary that we should read Psalm 82 fully:

The Psalm said that God stands in the congregation of the mighty and judges among 'gods'. The Psalmist questions how long these 'gods' will judge unjustly and accept the persons of the wicked. The following verses are instructions to defend the poor and fatherless, do justice to the afflicted and needy, and deliver the poor and needy and help them to get rid out of the hand of the wicked.

The 'gods' are supposed to render justice but if they do not do justice they are answerable to God. Many 'gods' have gone their own way rendering injustice to many and they are all accountable to the LORD. They are 'gods' and they are all the children of the most High, yet they shall all die like men and fall like one of the princes. Then Psalmist invokes God in prayer to judge the earth because He inherits al nations.

The question is who those 'gods' about whom Psalmist wrote are and about whom Jesus quoted in John Chapter 10:34-36

Hebrew Strong's Number 430 is " 'elohiym" is transliterated as "el-o-heem'"

1. Definition: (plural)
a. rulers, judges
b. divine ones
c. angels
d. gods
2. (plural intensive - singular meaning)
a. god, goddess
b. godlike one
c. works or special possessions of God
d. the (true) God
e. God

In KJV it is occurs 2606 times. In Genesis alone it occurs 189 times. Some of the verses where this word occurs in different contexts are as follows:

"In the beginning God created the heaven and the earth". (Genesis 1:1)

"For God doth know that in the day ye eat thereof, then your eyes shall be opened, and ye shall be as gods, knowing good and evil". (Genesis 3:5)

"Then his master shall bring him unto the judges; he shall also bring him to the door, or unto the door post; and his master shall bore his ear through with an aul; and he shall serve him for ever" (Exodus 21:6)

"If the thief be not found, then the master of the house shall be brought unto the judges, to see whether he have put his hand unto his neighbour's goods". (Exodus 22:8)

"For all manner of trespass, whether it be for ox, for ass, for sheep, for raiment, or for any manner of lost thing, which another challengeth to be his, the cause of both parties shall come before the judges; and whom the judges shall condemn, he shall pay double unto his neighbour" (Exodus 22:9).

In all the above verses 'elo-heem' is God, whose name is Jehovah, or the judges of Israel who were representatives of God on this earth. 2 Chronicles 19:6 shows that the judges in Israel were delivering judgments as representatives of God. Not all the judges delivered justice but few delivered injustice also. It is about those judges, who rendered injustice that the Psalmist wrote about.

"And said to the judges, Take heed what ye do: for ye judge not for man, but for the LORD, who is with you in the judgment". (2 Chronicles 19:6)

In Genesis 3:5 Serpent said that if Eve ate the forbidden fruit Eve and Adam will be like 'gods'. It is misinterpretation that the serpent was suggesting to eat the fruit in order that she and Adam may become like other 'gods', the agents of Satan, but the suggestion was that they will be like God knowing good and evil.

The word 'elo-heem' is used in plural. God is triune and this word was used to describe Him. When serpent said uttered this word to Eve, he was obviously saying to Eve that Adam and Eve (the two individuals) that they will be each like a God. It does not suggest that Serpent was saying to Eve that Adam and Eve will be like judges or like evil gods or rulers. Interpretation that they would like judges or evil rulers is gross misrepresentation to undermine the meaning of the word of God.

At this juncture there are also two phrases brought in to misrepresent the 'elo-heem' in order to bring in confusion that the 'gods' referred to in Psalm 82 and John 10 are some mystical "gods", who ruled on earth. The infusion of these two phrases is very appealing and interesting as if to project good knowledge of truth of Jesus.

The mystical figures are brought through assumptions to mislead the understanding of the deity of Lord Jesus Christ. The two phrases are: "HOST OF HEAVEN" and the "LORD of hosts". They come from some oblivion into the thoughts of those who want to undermine the deity of Lord Jesus Christ.

It should be understood that Jesus was not justifying in John 10:34-36 that Psalmist spoke of "Messiah" who was to come, but he was referring to earthly judges who rendered injustice and will face consequences of their deeds.

Jesus was pointing to Jews, the learned men, who alleged Him that He spoke blaspheme. Jesus quoted Psalm 82 to show that in the law that they knew of, it was written that "Ye are gods, and all of you are the children of the most High" and the verse is followed by the next verse which says: "But ye shall die like men, and fall like one of the princes" Those are all judges in

Israel who were the children of the most High appointed to render justice but failed in their duties as the children of the most High and the consequence is that they fall like one of the princes. They are not rulers over nations.

The phrase "HOST OF HEAVEN" is not used to represent evil gods or mystical figures, but they are stars and planets.

"Host" comes from Hebrew Strong's number 6635 which is transliterated as "Tsaba' ".

1. The definition is: that which goes forth, army, war, warfare, host

a. army, host
1. host (of organised army)
2. host (of angels)
3. of sun, moon, and stars
4. of whole creation
b. war, warfare, service, go out to war
c. service
"Heaven" comes from Hebrew Strong's number 8064 "Shamayim".
1. The definition is: heaven, heavens, sky
a. visible heavens, sky
1. as abode of the stars
2. as the visible universe, the sky, atmosphere, etc
b. Heaven (as the abode of God)

Stephen said: "Then God turned, and gave them up to worship the host of heaven; as it is written in the book of the prophets, O ye house of Israel, have ye offered to me slain beasts and sacrifices by the space of forty years in the wilderness?" (Acts 7:42)

The "host of heaven" mentioned in Acts 7:42 refers to stars and heavenly bodies, about which is written in the book of prophets.

"Except the LORD of hosts had left unto us a very small remnant, we should have been as Sodom, and we should have been like unto Gomorrah". (Isaiah 1:9)

Amos also wrote about the planet Saturn. "But ye have borne the tabernacle of your Moloch and Chiun your images, the star of your god, which ye made to yourselves". (Amos 5:26)

There is no reason to bring in "HOST OF HEAVEN' AND OR "Lord of HOSTS" into proving that Jesus deity is strengthened based on Psalm 82. These are misrepresentations and misinterpretations.

Jesus caught Jews, who were ready to stone Him to death alleging that He blasphemed God, in their own argument and intelligence and thwarted their presuppositions.

Note the argument Jesus placed.

• "If he called them 'gods', unto whom the word of God came"
 • "Say ye of him, whom the Father hath sanctified, and sent into the world, Thou blasphemest;"
 •"because I said, I am the Son of God?"

"If he called them gods, unto whom the word of God came, and the scripture cannot be broken; Say ye of him, whom the Father hath sanctified, and sent into the world, Thou blasphemest; because I said, I am the Son of God?" (John 10:35-36)

THE JUDGES AND THE JUDGEMENTS

God gave the children of Israel several instructions besides Ten Commandments. These instructions are rather explanations and elaborations of each commandment. Any one violating those instructions were judged and punished or provision for restitution is detailed. Perusal of few instructions and the judgments will give us understanding as to who these judges (otherwise called 'elo-heem' in Hebrew language) were and how they were judged during Old Testament period.

If an Israelite buys a Hebrew servant the servant can be in his home as slave for only six years and in the seventh year he should be released. But if the slave finds it good to serve his master more than the period he was supposed to be under him the master shall bring the slave before the judge to the door, and his master shall pierce the ear of the slave by an awl unto the doorpost. Then shall the slave serve his master for ever (Exodus 21:1-8).

A thief stealing an ox or sheep kills the animal he should restore at the rate of five oxen for one ox killed and four sheep for a sheep. If the thief is caught and he is killed there shall be no blood shed for him; but if it is during day time the thief shall be caught and delivered for judgment and restitution should be made to the one from whom the thief stole. If the restitution can not be made the thief shall be sold as slave. If the thief caught in action is killed during day time it shall be treated as murder. (Exodus 22:1-8)

If a man entices a maid, who was not betrothed yet, and lie with her, he shall surely endow her to be his wife, but if the father of the maid refuses to give the maid to him, he shall pay money according to the dowry of virgins. (Exodus 22:16-17)

The three examples shown above are only to give an idea how the justice system worked during Old Testament period and how the judges rendered justice or injustice. This is what is spoken of by the psalmist in Psalm 82. It was a Psalm of Asaph. He wrote that God who is the judge of all judges among the 'gods', that is the judges on this earth among the children of Israel. Remember these commandments and instructions were given to the children of Israel and not to Gentiles.

There is, therefore, no scope of application of these commandments or instructions to Gentiles and the scriptures are not speaking of some mystical figures or some strange gods, or idols, but the judges mentioned here are simply the judges whom the scriptures call as 'gods' among the children of Israel. Psalmist wrote about the judges who rendered injustice and became accountable to God, who is the judge of all. Psalmist calls for justice and invokes God's presence through his prayer that He may judge those judges ('gods'), who rendered injustice.

Jesus quotes those scriptures in John 10:34-36 and said that if scriptures, which can not be broken, call these human judges in Israel as 'gods' to whom the word of God came, what is wrong if He calls himself, who is sanctified and sent into the world, as the 'Son of God', and why would it be tantamount to blaspheming? He was not trying to establish his deity here nor was saying that Psalm 82 was a prophecy about him. He quoted these verses from Psalm 82 just as a rabbinical argument to win over the so-called intelligent Pharisees who were trying to trap him and stone him to death.

Jesus thwarted their intelligence in their own conceit and won the argument. He walked away unharmed in spite of their approach to stone him to death. No one could do any harm to Jesus before His appointed time. He offered himself when it was appointed time for him to lay His life and He took his life back when it was due time.

CHAPTER 13
INVITATION TO SALVATION

Today is the day of salvation. Please confess your sins to Jesus Christ and be blessed. Receive Salvation and eternal life. Jesus is the Way, the truth, and the life. Holy Bible says God created man, in his own image and named him as Adam and God put him in a very comfortable place called 'the garden of Eden' and gave him a wife, whom Adam named as Eve.

God gave Adam and Eve all the freedom except for eating the forbidden fruit, which Eve and Adam ate and brought sin into this world.

In order to redeem mankind from their sin God sent his one and only son, Jesus Christ, who died for our sake, was buried, rose from the dead and ascended in to heaven.

PROPHETS OF GOD AND FALSE PROPHETS

TRUE AND FALSE TAECHERS

ISBN-10:0989028380
ISBN-13:978-0-9890283-8-7

But there were false prophets also among the people, even as there shall be false teachers among you, who privily shall bring in damnable heresies, even denying the Lord that bought them, and bring upon themselves swift destruction. And many shall follow their pernicious ways; by reason of whom the way of truth shall be evil spoken of. (2 Peter 2:1-2)

There are many Bible teachers in the world and it is hard to differentiate the true teachings of Lord Jesus Christ and false teachings from the Adversary, the Satan. Bible says in the last days there will be many false prophets and false teachers leading astray the innocents from the truth.

Bible asks us to test who is of the Lord and who is not.

WHO IS OF GOD AND WHO IS NOT?

"Wherefore I give you to understand, that no man speaking by the Spirit of God calleth Jesus accursed: and that no man can say that Jesus is the Lord, but by the Holy Ghost" 1 Corinthians 12:3)

This Book deals with the subject of True and False teachers

About the Author:

Hailing from India and born in a Christian middle class family, the author was raised in a Christian background and had education in Christian Institutions. The author accepted Lord Jesus Christ as his personal savior when he was a boy of 13 and he is a naturalized citizen of United States of America. The author is a postgraduate in English language and literature.

This then was the message that he heard of the Son of God, Lord Jesus Christ.

LESLIE M. JOHN

www.ingramcontent.com/pod-product-compliance
Lightning Source LLC
Chambersburg PA
CBHW061722020426
42331CB00006B/1049